THE MILFORD SERI
POPULAR WRITERS OF TODAY
ISSN 0163-2469
VOLUME SIXTY-THREE

The Impact of Stephen King on Popular Culture

*Second Edition,
Revised and Expanded*

by

Michael R. Collings
Pepperdine University

A Thaddeus Dikty Book

BORGO PRESS / WILDSIDE PRESS

www.wildsidepress.com

Library of Congress Cataloging-in-Publication Data

Collings, Michael R.
  Scaring us to death : the impact of Stephen King on popular culture / by
Michael R. Collings. — 2nd ed., rev. and expanded.
  p. cm. — (The Milford series. Popular writers of today, ISSN 0163-2469 ;
v. 63)
  "A Thaddeus Dikty book."
  Includes bibliographical references (p.) and index.
  ISBN 0-930261-37-2 (cloth). — ISBN 0-930261-38-0 (pbk.)
  1. King, Stephen, 1947- —Criticism and interpretation. 2. Popular
culture—United States—History—20th century. 3. Horror tales, American—
History and criticism. 4. King, Stephen, 1947- —Influence. I. Title. II.
Series.
PS3561.I483Z626 1997   95-5023
813'.54—dc20   CIP

SECOND EDITION

CONTENTS

YOU, STEPHEN KING

You, Stephen King,
Smiling behind Coke-bottle lenses,
Bushy beard, New England dialect,

And sixty-million copies of your words

How does it work that you,
So distant and removed
(We shared a table once in a hotel bar
But I know you no more now
Than then)
Can touch the deep-springs of *my* fears?

The strongest human coil is fear—
And when its tensions birth
They tear through bowel and gut
Erupt an alien spray
Adrenalin and blood

Fear—

And more.

I cried, you know,
When Stella Flanders crossed the Reach.
I tried to read it to my wife.
We sat beneath the elms
Where the scratch of rusty lawn-swing hinges
Echoed an early sparrow's song—
I read cold death,
Ravenous cancers,
Immutable ice.
The sparrow sang, but the hinges strangled
Into silence.
We stopped.
Stella saw the cap—
My voice broke like too-thin ice
Along a rushing river's bank—a lacy rime

That cannot bear....

I cried. She finished reading
When my voice thawed
And waters gushed beneath
And through the ice.

Stella Flanders crossed the reach,
Reached across to slip her icy fingernail
Along my grandmother's withered neck,
A point of blood welling
Where the cold laid siege
To blood-press ninety years and more.
And the waters thawed and gushed
Beneath my voice.

When ghosts join hands and sing of joy
The coils of fear
Petal
Like the first elusive rose
Of June.

—Michael R. Collings
Thousand Oaks, California

A STEPHEN KING CHRONOLOGY

Abbreviations used in this chronology:

(anth.)—Anthology
(coll.)—Collection
(n)—Novel
(s)—Short story
(nonf.)—Nonfiction
(p)—Poem

1947   Stephen Edwin King born on September 21, in Portland, Maine, the second son of Donald and Nellie Ruth (Pillsbury) King (King's older brother, David Victor King, was adopted two years before King's birth).

1949   Donald King walks out the door and is never heard from again. Over the next nine years, the King family lives in Scarborough, New York; Croton-on-Hudson, New York; Chicago, Illinois; West De Pere, Wisconsin; Fort Wayne, Indiana; and Stratford, Connecticut (see David King's "Growing Up with the Boogeyman," in *The Shape Under the Sheet*, by Stephen J. Spignesi, p. 31-38).

1957   In October, when King first hears that the Russians orbited Sputnik, he is struck by the implicit terror in the announcement, initiating a life-long concern for the blending of horror and technology.

1958   King, his mother, and his brother move to Durham, Maine, in the fall of 1958; King remains there until he completes his college education. King meets Chris Chesley.

1960   Publishes *People, Places, Things* (coll., with Chris Chesley; self-published through Triad Publishing Company).

1963   Publishes a second printing of *People, Places, Things* (coll., with Chris Chesley). Begins study at the Lisbon Falls High School.

1964   Publishes "The Star Invaders" (s; self-published through Triad, Inc.).

1965   Publishes "I Was a Teenage Grave Robber" (s), his first semi-professional publication.

1966   King begins study as a freshman at the University of Maine, Orono, majoring in English. "I Was A Teenage Grave Robber" reprinted as "In a Half-World of Terror" (s).

1967   Publishes "The Glass Floor" (s), in *Startling Mystery Stories*—his first professional sale. Completes the manuscript for *The Long Walk* (published in 1979).

1968   Publishes "Here There Be Tygers" (s), "Cain Rose Up" (s), "Strawberry Spring" (s); "Harrison State Park '68" (p). Begins work on a novel-length manuscript, *Sword in the Darkness*.

1969   Publishes "Night Surf" (s), "The Reaper's Image" (s), "Stud City"; "Garbage Truck" columns (nonf., through 1970); "The Dark Man" (p).

1970   Graduates from UMO with a B.Sc. degree in English. Begins work in a number of menial jobs, including laborer in an industrial laundry and pumping gas at a filling station. Publishes "Slade" (s), "Graveyard Shift" (s); "A Possible Fairy Tale" (nonf.); "Donovan's Brain" (p), "Silence" (p). Completes manuscript for *Blaze*, an unpublished novel.

1971   Marries Tabitha Spruce, a fellow student at UMO, on January 2, 1971. Birth of first child, Naomi Rachel. Publishes "The Blue Air Compressor" (s), "I Am the Doorway" (s); Untitled poem, "Brooklyn August" (p), "The Hardcase Speaks" (p). Completes the manuscript for *The Running Man* (published 1981), his fourth novel manuscript. Begins teaching at Hampden Academy, a position he holds for two years. Begins submitting novels to Doubleday.

1972   Publishes "Suffer the Little Children" (s), "The Fifth Quarter" (s, as "JOHN SWITHEN"), "Battleground" (s), "The Mangler" (s). Begins work on a short story that would ultimately evolve into *Carrie* (published 1974).

1973   Birth of first son, Joseph Hill. Publishes "The Boogeyman" (s), "Trucks" (s), "Gray Matter" (s), "It Grows on You" (s); "The

7

Horror Market Writer and the Ten Bears" (nonf.). In March, submits *Carrie* to Doubleday; the novel is accepted. Begins work on *Second Coming,* an early version of *'Salem's Lot* (published 1975). Nellie King (Stephen's mother) dies of cancer.

1974   Publishes *Carrie* (n); "Sometimes They Come Back" (s). Completes work on *'Salem's Lot* and *Roadwork* (published 1981). Moves to Boulder, CO and begins writing *The Stand* and *The Shining.*

1975   The King family returns to Maine. King publishes *'Salem's Lot* (n); "The Lawnmower Man" (s), "The Revenge of Lardass Hogan" (s); "Writing a First Novel" (nonf.). Completes the manuscript for *The Stand.*

1976   Publishes "Weeds" (s), "The Ledge" (s), "I Know What You Need" (s); "Not Guilty" (nonf.). *Carrie* released as a feature-length film directed by Brian de Palma, giving King's novels increased visibility and interest.

1977   Publishes *The Shining* (n); *Rage* (n, as "RICHARD BACHMAN"); "The Cat from Hell," (s), "Children of the Corn" (s), "One for the Road" (s), "The Man Who Loved Flowers" (s). Completes drafts of *The Dead Zone, Firestarter,* and *Cujo.* Travels to England and meets Peter Straub; first discussions of a collaboration that would lead to *The Talisman.*

1978   Birth of second son, Owen Phillip. Publishes *The Stand* (n), a difficult book that he has described as his "own little Vietnam"; *Night Shift* (coll.); *Stephen King* (coll.); "The Night of the Tiger" (s), "The Gunslinger" (s), "Man with a Belly" (s), "Nona" (s); "The Fright Report" (nonf.); *"The Doll Who Ate His Mother"* (nonf.). Serves as Writer-in-Residence, UMO. Judge for the 1977 World Fantasy Awards.

1979   Publishes *The Dead Zone* (n); *The Long Walk* (n, as "RICHARD BACHMAN"); "The Crate" (s); "How to Scare a Woman to Death" (nonf.); "The Writing Life" (nonf.); "The Horrors of '79" (nonf.). Completes drafts for *Christine, Pet Sematary,* and *Danse Macabre*; completes screenplay for *Creepshow.* Guest of Honor, World Fantasy Convention. Receives World Fantasy Award nominations for *The Stand, Night Shift.* *'Salem's Lot* airs as a three-night mini-series for television.

1980   The King family moves to Bangor, ME, where they purchase a Victorian mansion. Publishes *Firestarter* (n; first limited edition publication); "The Way Station" (s), "The Wedding Gig" (s), "Big Wheels: A Tale of the Laundry Game" (s), "The Monkey" (s), "Crouch End" (s), "The Mist" (s); "A Pilgrim's Progress" (nonf.); "On Becoming a Brand Name" (nonf.), "Books" (nonf.), "Imagery and the Third Eye" (nonf.), "Some Notes on *Tales of the Vampyre*" (nonf.). Completes first draft of *IT*.
      ' Becomes the first American writer to have three books on the national bestsellers lists simultaneously: *Firestarter, The Dead Zone,* and *The Shining*. Release of Stanley Kubrick's film adaptation of *The Shining*.

1981   Publishes *Cujo* (n); *Roadwork* (n, as "RICHARD BACHMAN"); *Stephen King's Danse Macabre* (nonf.); "The Oracle and the Mountain" (s), "The Jaunt" (s), "The Slow Mutants" (s), "The Monster in the Closet" (excerpt from *Cujo*), "The Bird and the Album" (excerpt from *IT*), "Do the Dead Sing?" (s), "The Gunslinger and the Dark Man," (s), "The Man Who Would Not Shake Hands" (s); "When Is TV Too Scary for Children?" (nonf.), "The Cannibal and the Cop" (nonf.), "The Sorry State of TV Shows" (nonf.).
      Receives Career Alumni Award from the University of Maine, Orono. Cameo appearance in George A. Romero's *Knightriders*. Publication of Edward J. Zagorski's *Teacher's Manual: Stephen King*.

1982   Publishes *The Dark Tower: The Gunslinger* (coll.); *The Running Man* (n, as "RICHARD BACHMAN"); *The Plant* (excerpt from novel-in-progress); *Creepshow* (coll.); *Different Seasons* (coll.); "The Raft" (s), "Before the Play" (s), "Skybar" (s), "Survivor Type" (s); "Between Rock and a Hard Place" (nonf.), "Visit with an Endangered Species" (nonf.), "The Ludlum Attraction" (nonf.); "Mentors" (nonf.); "Favorite Films" (nonf.), "Digging the Boogens" (nonf.), "On *The Shining* and Other Perpetrations" (nonf.), "Peter Straub: An Appreciation" (nonf.), "Horrors!" (nonf.), "*The Evil Dead*: Why You Haven't Seen It Yet...And Why You Ought To" (nonf.), "My High School Horrors" (nonf.). Begins work on *The Talisman,* with Peter Straub, and *The Cannibals*. Completes work on *Thinner* (published 1984).
      Receives the Hugo award for best nonfiction of the year, for *Danse Macabre*. Receives the World Fantasy Award for "Do the Dead Sing?" Named Best Fiction Writer of the Year in a poll by *Us Magazine*. Writes screenplay for

Creepshow. Release of *Creepshow*, directed by George A. Romero; King has a cameo appearance. Publication of Tim Underwood and Chuck Miller's *Fear Itself: The Horror Fiction of Stephen King*. Publication of Douglas E. Winter's critique, *Stephen King*.

1983   Publishes *Christine* (n); *Cycle of the Werewolf* (n); *Pet Sematary* (n); *The Plant, Part Two* (excerpt from novel-in-progress); "The Word Processor of the Gods" (s), "Uncle Otto's Truck" (s), "The Return of Timmy Baterman" (excerpt from *Pet Sematary*); "Don't be Cruel" (nonf.), "Dear Walden People" (nonf.), "Horrors!" (nonf.), "A Profile of Robert Bloch" (nonf.), "Ross Thomas Stirs the Pot" (nonf.), "Berni Wrightson" (nonf.), "Black Magic and Music" (nonf.), "Last Waltz" (nonf.), "Special Makeup Effects and the Writer" (nonf.); "Stephen King," in *A Gift from Maine* (nonf.), "Stephen King's 10 Favorite Horror Books or Short Stories" (nonf.). Completes drafts of three novels: *The Talisman*, *The Tommyknockers*, and *The Napkins* (later retitled *The Eyes of the Dragon*). Completes the screenplay for *Cat's Eye*.

Presents "An Evening with Stephen King at the Billerica, Massachusetts, Public Library." Release of John Carpenter's film adaptation of *Christine*. Release of Lewis Teague's film adaptation of *Cujo*. Release of David Cronenberg's film adaptation of *The Dead Zone*. Release of videocassette versions of "The Boogeyman" and "The Woman in the Room."

1984   Publishes *The Eyes of the Dragon* (n, Philtrum limited edition); *The Talisman* (n), with Peter Straub; *Thinner* (n, as "RICHARD BACHMAN"); "Gramma" (s), "Mrs. Todd's Shortcut" (s), "The Ballad of the Flexible Bullet" (s), "The Revelations of 'Becka Paulson" (excerpt from *The Tommyknockers*); "The Irish King" (nonf.), "1984: A Bad Year If You Fear Friday the 13th" (nonf.), "Dr. Seuss and the Two Faces of Fantasy" (nonf.), "Why I Am for Gary Hart" (nonf.), "My First Car" (nonf.), articles and reviews.

Presents Guest of Honor Address, "Dr. Seuss and the Two Faces of Fantasy," International Conference on the Fantastic in the Arts, Boca Raton FL, March 24. Appearance in American Express commercial for television. Release of Fritz Kiersch's film adaptation of *Children of the Corn*. Release of Mark Lester's film adaptation of *Firestarter*. Publication of James Van Hise's *Enterprise Incidents Presents Stephen King*. Publication of Douglas E. Winter's *Stephen King: The Art of Darkness*.

1985 Acknowledges that "RICHARD BACHMAN" is Stephen King. Publishes *Skeleton Crew* (coll.); *Silver Bullet* (coll.); *The Bachman Books* (coll.); *The Plant, Part Three*; "Heroes for Hope: Starring the X-Men"; "Dolan's Cadillac" (s), "Beachworld" (s); "What Went Down When Magyk Went Up" (nonf.), "Theodore Sturgeon" (nonf.), "King Testifies" (nonf.), "Cat from Hell" (nonf.), "The Politics of Limited Editions" (nonf.), "His Creepiest Movies" (nonf.), "Lists That Matter" (nonf.), "Ghostmaster General" (nonf.), "The King Speaks" (nonf.), "Why I Was Bachman" (nonf.), "What Ails the U. S. Male" (nonf.), "My Say" (nonf.), "*Regis Reprimandum*" (nonf.).

Establishes another record with five titles on the national bestsellers lists simultaneously, November 1985-January 1986: *Skeleton Crew* (hardcover), *The Bachman Books* (hardcover), *The Talisman* (mass-market paper), *The Bachman Books* (mass-market paper), *Thinner* (mass-market paper). Writes final screenplays for *Cat's Eye* and *Silver Bullet*. Release of Lewis Teague's *Cat's Eye*, with screenplay by King. Release of Daniel Attias's *Silver Bullet*. Appearance of "The Word Processor of the Gods" on the *Tales from the Darkside* television series. Presents "An Evening with Stephen King," at the University of Massachusettts, Amherst. Guest of Honor, Third Annual World Drive-in Movie Festival and Custom Car Rally. First issue of *Castle Rock: The Stephen King Newsletter* published in January, 1985; newsletter continues through the end of 1989.

Publication of Darrell Schweitzer's *Discovering Stephen King*. Publication of Michael R. Collings and David A. Engebretson's *The Shorter Works of Stephen King*. Publication of Michael R. Collings's *Stephen King as Richard Bachman* and *The Many Facets of Stephen King*.

1986 Publishes *IT* (n); "For the Birds" (s); "Lists that Matter" (nonf.), "Let's Scare Dick and Jane" (nonf.), "Tough Talk and Tootsies" (nonf.), "King vs. Chalker: One Last Round" (nonf.), "Say 'No' to the Enforcers" (nonf.), "Everything You Need to Know About Writing Successfully—in Ten Minutes" (nonf.), "Stephen King Comments on *IT*" (nonf.), "On *The Far Side*" (nonf.), "How *IT* Happened" (nonf.), "Write-In" (nonf.), "Big Jim Thompson: An Appreciation," "The Dreaded X" (nonf.), articles about baseball and the Red Sox.

Screenwrites and directs *Maximum Overdrive*. Release of *Maximum Overdrive*, with a cameo appearance by King. Release of Rob Reiner's film adaptation of "The Body," *Stand By Me*. King acts as Guest VJ for MTV, June 27. Appearance of "Gramma" as an episode on the *Twilight Zone* television series. Presents "Banned Books and Other Concerns: The Virginia Beach Lecture," Virginia Beach, VA, September 22. Lloyd Elliot Lecturer in English, University of Maine. Publication of Michael R. Collings's *The Films of Stephen King*. Publication of Jessie Horsting's *Stephen King: At the Movies*. Publication of Michael R. Collings's *The Annotated Guide to Stephen King*. Publication of Tim Underwood and Chuck Miller's *Kingdom of Fear: The World of Stephen King*.

1987   Publishes *The Eyes of the Dragon* (n, mass-market edition); *Misery* (n); *The Tommyknockers* (n); *The Dark Tower II: The Drawing of the Three* (coll.); "The Doctor's Case" (s), "Popsy" (s); "Postscript to *Overdrive*" (nonf.), "Whining About the Movies in Bangor" (nonf.), "Turning the Thumbscrews on the Reader" (nonf.), "On John D. MacDonald" (nonf.), "Entering the Rock Zone" (nonf.), articles on baseball and the Red Sox.

Appears on the annual hardcover fiction bestsellers lists with three titles: *The Tommyknockers* (#1), *Misery* (#4), and *The Eyes of the Dragon* (#10). Release of *Creepshow 2,* directed by Michael Gornick and adapted for screen by George A. Romero. Appearance of "Sorry, Right Number" as an episode on *Tales from the Darkside*. Release of *Return to Salem's Lot,* a film based loosely on King's novel. Presents lecture, "Friends of the Andre Dubus Library Series," Boston MA, March 1. Delivers Commencement Address, University of Maine, May 6. Publication of Michael R. Collings's *The Stephen King Phenomenon*, Jeff Conner's *Stephen King Goes to Hollywood*, and Gary Hoppenstand and Ray B. Browne's *The Gothic World of Stephen King*.

1988   Publishes *Nightmares in the Sky: Gargoyles and Grotesques* (nonf.); "Night Flier" (s), "The Reploids" (s), "Sneakers" (s), "Dedication" (s); "The Ideal, Genuine Writer: A Forenote" (nonf.), "'Ever Et Raw Meat? and Other Weird Questions" (nonf.), "This Guy is *Really* Scary" (nonf.), "SK Criticized for References to Blacks: Stephen King Replies" (nonf.), "SK Clarifies Gardner Reference" (nonf.), "The Ultimate Catalogue" (nonf.), "Robert Marasco: *Burnt Offerings*" (nonf.), reviews and articles on baseball, etc.

Receives Bram Stoker Award (Horror Writers of America) for *Misery* (co-recipient with Robert R. McCammon). *Carrie* adapted as a stage musical; performed in England and New York. *Rage* adapted as a stage play. Release of

Paul Michael Glaser's film adaptation of *The Running Man.* Publication of Joseph Reino's *Stephen King: The First Decade....* Publication of Tony Magistrale's *Landscape of Fear.* Publication of Tim Underwood and Chuck Miller's *Bare Bones.* Publication of Don Herron's *Reign of Fear.*

1989 Publishes *The Dark Half* (n); *Dolan's Cadillac* (s)*; My Pretty Pony* (s); "Rainy Season" (s), "Home Delivery" (s). Writes screenplay for *Pet Sematary* film. Release of *Pet Sematary,* with a cameo appearqance by King.
    Bram Stoker Award nominations for "Night Flier" and "Dedication." Delivers publiç lecture, 1989 Authors Series, Pasadena, CA, April 26. Publication of Tyson Blue's *The Unseen King,* Don Herron's *Feast of Fear,* George Beahm's *The Stephen King Companion,* and *Das Stephen King Buch.*

1990 Publishes *The Stand: Complete and Uncut Edition* (n); *Four Past Midnight* (coll.); "The Moving Finger" (s); "The Bear" (s). Release of *Tales from the Darkside: The Movie* [which includes "The Cat from Hell" segment based on King's short story]; release of *Stephen King's Graveyard Shift* by Paramount Pictures, October 26, 1990; release of *Misery* by Castle Rock Entertainment, November 30, 1990. The mini-series TV adaptation of *IT* aired, November 18 and November 20, 1990.
    Guest, Portland Public Library Centennial, Portland, Maine. March 1990. Publication of Stephen Spignesi's *The Stephen King Quiz Book,* James Van Hise's *Stephen King and Clive Barker: The Illustrated Guide to the Masters of the Macabre,* Carroll F. Terrell's *Stephen King: Man and Artist.*

1991 Publishes *The Dark Tower III: The Waste Lands* (n); *Needful Things* (n). Television presentations of *Stephen King's "Sometimes They Come Back"* (made-for-TV film) and *Stephen King's Golden Years* (miniseries).
    Guest, ABA Convention, June, 1991. Publication of George Beahm's *The Stephen King Story: A Literary Profile; Gauntlet 2: Exploring the Limits of Free Expression* (Stephen King Special Issue), edited by Barry Hoffman; Stephen Spignesi's *The Shape Under the Sheet: The Complete Stephen King Encyclopedia; The Shining Reader,* edited by Anthony Magistrale; Carroll F. Terrell's *Stephen King: Man and Artist* (revised edition).

1992 Publishes *Gerald's Game* (n). Release of *Stephen King's Sleepwalkers* (film); *The Lawnmower Man* (film), a motion picture so distanced from King's original story that attempts were made to have his name removed from the credits.

Publication of George Beahm's *The Stephen King Story: A Literary Profile—Updated and Revised*; Anthony Magistrale's *Stephen King: The Second Decade, Danse Macabre to The Dark Half*; Magistrale's *The Dark Descent: Essays Defining Stephen King's Horrorscape*; Anne Saidman's *Stephen King*; Stephen Spignesi's *Second Stephen King Quiz Book*.

1993   Publishes *Dolores Claiborne* (n); *Nightmares & Dreamscapes* (coll.). Release of *The Tommyknockers* (made-for-television film). Publication of Stephen Spignesi's *Stephen King A to Z: A Dictionary of People, Places, and Things in the Works of the King of Horror*; and Spignesi's *The Complete Stephen King Encyclopedia: The Definitive Guide to the Works of America's Master of Horror* (paperback reprint of *The Shape Under the Sheet*).

1994   Publishes *Insomnia* (n). Release of *The Stand* (made-for-television film); *The Shawshank Redemption* (film); *Dolores Claiborne* (film). Publication of *Demon-Driven: Stephen King and the Art of Writing*, edited by George Beahm (signed, limited edition also 1994).

1995   Publishes *Rose Madder* (n). Release of *The Langoliers* (made-for-television film). "The Man in the Black Suit" wins a World Fantasy Award for Best Short Fiction and the O. Henry Award for Best American Short Story.

1996   Publishes *The Green Mile*, a six-volume serial novel (March-August); *Desperation* (n); *The Regulators*, by "RICHARD BACHMAN" (n). Production of *The Night Flier*, *Thinner*, and *The Shining* as films/teleplays. Publication of *The Work of Stephen King*, by Michael R. Collings.

1997   Publishes *The Dark Tower IV: Wizard and Glass*.

I.

A CONCATENATION OF MONSTERS: STEPHEN KING'S *IT*

This chapter incorporates two responses to *IT*, arguably one of King's seminal works and by his own account a transitional novel in his canon. The first expands and revises an open letter to King published with his answer in *Castle Rock: The Stephen King Newsletter* in July, 1986; the second was presented in a slightly different form at the annual meeting of the Philological Association of the Pacific Coast (PAPC), held in November 1986 at the University of California, Riverside. Part of the session on Folklore and Mythology in literature, the paper was read in conjunction with one study outlining pre-Hellenic and Sanskrit versions of the myth of the goddess born from the sea foam, and another analyzing the cultural preconceptions underlying an Eskimo folk tale.

This chapter fills two functions. First, it responds to one of King's most important novels, the novel that he has himself referred to as culminating one stage in his career. And second, it illustrates the broad base of interest King's work can generate—ranging from a specialty (some might argue fan-oriented) newsletter to a session in an academic conference that has an almost ninety-year history of involvement with criticism and scholarship.

1. *IT*: Stephen King's Comprehensive Masterpiece

Reading *IT*, one becomes more aware of how completely the novel functions as a compendium of horror, a self-reflexive work that looks back not only to literary traditions but to film, folklore, and to King's own novels and stories.

On one level, *IT* is intensely autobiographical. The fact that King was eleven in 1958 (as are most of his characters) explains much of the power of the novel—and much of its historical fascination for me, since I was also eleven in 1958. One of the central characters, Bill Denbrough, is a successful writer of horror novels, several of which have been turned into films. His early experiences with creative writing in college sound as if they might parallel King's own: "Here is a poor boy from the state of Maine who goes to the University on a

15

scholarship. All his life he wanted to be a writer, but when he enrolls in the writing courses he finds himself lost without a compass in a strange and frightening land." As King consistently does, Denbrough asserts the primacy of story as story: "Why does a story have to be socio-anything? Politics...culture...history...aren't those natural ingredients in any story, if it's told well?... I mean can't you guys just let a story be a story?" (*IT*, 125). The passages describing Denbrough's struggles do not, of course, project King's own experiences exactly; instead, they suggest and tantalize, while carrying a distinctive ring of authenticity that deepens Denbrough's character and prepares him for the test to come.

In fact, connections between King, his world, and his novel are at times so close that one of the minor characters who suffers a dramatic death by dismemberment, Eddie King, not only carries a variant on King's name (Stephen Edwin King) but is described as a bearded man wearing glasses almost as thick as his stomach. Several episodes reflect actual occurrences in Bangor; the murder of a homosexual in "After the Festival" is "almost literally true...the names have been changed to protect the innocent (not to mention the guilty...), but what happened in Derry happened in Bangor two summers ago." Even more directly,

> ...Derry 1958 is Stratford, Connecticut, where I was eleven. That's where The Barrens were, and Eddie Kasbrak (when we moved back to Maine his last words to me were, "I guess that's all, bastard-ball!"), and Mr. Nell, who used to buy my brother and me apple pie a la mode at the Stratford Diner. There was a dam in The Barrens; my brother showed us how to build it, and yeah, the cops showed up, Mr. Nell among them.[1]

More intriguingly, however, *IT* incorporates references to many of King's major fictions, particularly in the central characters. Stan Uris lives in Atlanta, close enough to the locale of *Firestarter* to be suggestive. Richie lives as an adult in California and is part of the "in" culture of rock 'n roll, just as was Larry Underwood in *The Stand* ("Stan Underwood" appears briefly at the end of the novel). Ben Hanscomb lives near Gatlin and Hemingford Home, Nebraska, familiar as the setting for "Children of the Corn" and a key landscape in *The Stand*. Eddie Kraspback is from New York, also important in *The Stand*. And Bill Denbrough's temporary home in England suggests *The Talisman*, although peripherally; Peter Straub was living in England when he and King first met and discussed collaborating. In an additional layering, *IT* reflects the recurrent evil portrayed in Straub's *Floating Dragon*; some readers have in fact mentioned *Floating*

Dragon, *The Talisman*, and *IT* as comprising a Straub/King triptych of horror.

Mike Hanlon has remained in Derry, which is, as noted, an analogue to the towns King knew as a child. Derry is explicitly related to Stratford, Connecticut; Bangor, Maine; and the University of Maine at Orono, locales with which King was familiar—and certainly the name Hanlon at least hints at "Hatlen," the name of King's English professor at UMO. In a curious coincidence, "Hanlon" also repeats the key name in *Invasion* (by "Aaron Wolfe," a pseudonym for Dean Koontz), which was for a time discussed as being by King.

About a third of the way through *IT*, King moves back in time to 1930 and the burning of a black servicemen's club. To one alert to the reflexive nature of the novel, it comes as no surprise that one hero of the disaster—credited with saving many lives—is a young army cook who somehow seems to *know* what to do and when to do it...named Dick Hallorann. The monstrous black bird that plays an important role in the episode may be a visual parallel to the manta-like black form that erupts from the Presidential Suite of the Overlook Hotel in the final pages of *The Shining*. And it may be particularly significant that only Dick Hallorann sees it.

Later, as *IT* moves to its climax, a character hitches a ride with a ghostly revenant from his past...in (again, no surprise) a red and white 1958 Plymouth Fury.

On a more abstract, thematic level, *IT* continues the exploration of childhood and maturity begun in such stories as "The Body" and "The Raft"; of the conflict between childhood and the adult world implicit in such works as *Rage*, *The Long Walk*, "Here There Be Tygers," and "Cain Rose Up"; of the inimical relationships between parent and child at the center of *Carrie*, *Cujo*, and *Pet Sematary*; and of childhood beliefs in monsters come true, as in *'Salem's Lot* and *Cycle of the Werewolf*.

This last also suggests the wide-ranging experimentation in *IT*, as King introduces almost every horror monster—literary and filmic—that has found place in our culture. The werewolf appears in references to *I Was a Teenage Werewolf*, along with the Mummy, the walking dead, Lovecraftian horrors from distant places ("The Colour Out of Space"), a crawling eye (*The Crawling Eye*), and assorted giant birds, piranha, parasites, etc. Images from the film *Alien* appear, as do allusions to a number of the 1950s' films King has noted as being influential in his development.

Not content with including creatures, King also introduces contemporaries into the novel. As one character checks out a book from the Derry library, he notes that it had been checked out only three times in the past twenty-seven years—by Charles Brown, David G. Hartwell, and Joseph Payne Brennan. The first two are SF/Fantasy publishers, and the third is the author of "Slime," which King has mentioned as a background to "The Raft." Later, another David Hartwell appears in the novel.

Shirley Jackson receives attention in a reference to Hill House. Similarly, H. P. Lovecraft provides much of the underlying imagery for *IT*. Indeed, *IT* may be one of King's most Lovecraftian novels. Although the monster also suggests Tolkien's Shelob at critical moments, It also brings to mind Lovecraft's eldritch alien species. References to alien, non-Euclidian geometry, to "rugose horrors," and to entities from a larger universe at best disinterested in (at worst inimical to) humanity illustrate King's deep debt to Lovecraft.

IT also continues King's exploration of important themes, especially his reconsideration of the sacrificial child. A number of critics have traced this theme in much that King has written, particularly prior to 1985: the child forced to confront the adult world without any support or understanding. Beginning with *Rage*, King has continually pitted the innocent world of the child against the harsh, cynical, hypocritical world of adults...usually to the detriment of the child, as in *Carrie*, *The Shining*, *Cujo*, "The Body," "Apt Pupil," "The Raft," and others.

In *IT*, however, King's fictional children grow up. And along the way to maturity, there is sacrifice aplenty, in 1958, 1985, and the other years in which the cycle of horror crests. Throughout the bloody history of It in Derry, children have been the primary target—It feeds on them, literally as It consumes their flesh, and figuratively as It absorbs their fear and terror. But in this novel—really for the first time in a novel-length work from King—the sacrifice of the child succeeds.

In earlier fictions, there was a lingering sense that the death or threatened death of the child was ultimately of little value. Nothing changes after Carrie White's death; a final scene suggests that the telekinetic powers are already at work again, presumably destroying other innocents. In *'Salem's Lot*, the best one can hope for is to escape; the ostensible heroine dies and the child loses family and heritage. In *The Stand*, one of the closest approaches to a fully optimistic novel King has yet written, there is renewed peace; but the Dark Man still exists, as do those bombs and weapons of destruction left deserted (and in the *Complete & Uncut Edition*, even this illusion of peace is shattered in the restored final chapter). A similar pattern concludes *The Eyes of the Dragon* as the evil magician disappears and must be hunted by the repentant foolish prince; the text suggests that readers may have to wait for the completed Dark Tower saga before the conflicts set in motion in *The Eyes of the Dragon* fully cease. "The Mist" certainly ends without much hope—so little that King is forced to express that small sense of possibility explicitly in the final words, "hope and Hartford." And with *Cujo*, *Christine*, *Thinner*, and superlatively in *Pet Sematary*, there is almost no chance that the child's death will result in anything but continuing horror (even if delayed, as in *Christine*).

Only rarely does the child become instrumental in restoring order. It might be argued that *The Shining* concludes optimistically—although even within the limits of the text Danny Torrance is just beginning to break free of his experience, and the other levels of sacrificial children (the Gradys, even Jack and Wendy themselves) have brought forth little good. More critically, however, the *source* of evil is not destroyed, as Hallorann realizes when the great black shape emerges from the Presidential Suite just before the Overlook explodes. As happens so often in King's fiction, "the horrific elements, though displaced, survive, and in their survival lies the kernal of future horror."[1]

In "The Word Processor of the Gods," the child dies—and from that death comes justice in an unjust world. If one assumes that the "true" son is not killed but simply deleted and thus in some sense never existed, "Word Processor of the Gods" *does* end positively, a conclusion exceeded to that point only by "The Reach" in optimism.

IT breaks with the typical pattern in King's prose. Instead of irresolute closure, there is a clear sense that evil has indeed been destroyed. On a literal level as well as a symbolic level, King is careful to point out that It has been defeated; while the mechanisms of It's defeat are not new to King's fictions, the *fact* of that defeat is.

In part, the sense of absolute closure relates to two key developments: first, King overtly acknowledges an "Other" to counter the force of evil, a point suggested in *The Stand* and not fully developed intil the conclusion of *Needful Things*; and second, he has finally reconciled the worlds of children and adults, paradoxically by having children act as adults (a common motif elsewhere in his fiction) *and* by having adults become as children. The characters return as adults to the sewers beneath Derry, signaling their acceptance of adult responsibility and of childhood faith combined into an irresistible force.

Because of It's relationship to the children-become-adults, Pennywise the Clown stands among King's most ambitious "monsters." Like Satan in Milton's *Paradise Lost*, the character is ubiquitous, powerful, seductive, and fatally convincing in It's many guises. And, also like Satan in the same poem, It receives much of King's attention—and some of the novel's best lines. Although the monster's multiple manifestations do tend toward the expected (given the length of the novel and the many appearances It makes, however, that sense is almost inevitable), often described in similar terms (but again, how many ways are there to express absolute horror?), they form the core of the novel. As the children discover the nature of their enemy, and their adult selves rediscover painfully it, Pennywise grows into a monster strong enough and secure enough in evil to provide more than a strawman or cardboard opponent. There may be momentary drops in horror, as when we discover It's "real" form, since for some readers the spider-entity seems stereotypic and trite. Still, King had to select a single manifestation for the climactic confrontation; and since any one he chose might prove less frightening than others for some of his readership, a lessening of emotional conviction was probably inevitable. But that drop is more than made up for as King takes us into the mind of It and reveals It's relation to the "macrouniverse."

Unfortunately, that revelation leads King into the same difficulty that Milton faced in *Paradise Lost*: the threat that his villain might become larger than his hero—or, in King's case, his multiple heroes. King counters the threat by setting seven characters opposite It, seven being an appropriately mystical number of great potency. Later, the number drops to five, less powerful than seven but still a number with substantial mystical/magical significance. The important point, though, is that the heroic role is divided and that each character plays a critical part in destroying It. Milton resolved his dilemma in *Paradise Lost* by dividing his later attention between the Son in the early books and Adam and Eve in the Garden in the later books; King largely restricts his interest to human spheres, so the further subdivisions become necessary. Still, given the intensively re-created backgrounds King gives us for each of the seven, we believe that they *will* in fact be a match for It...almost.

That "almost" is important because in *IT* (again, for almost the first time in King's fiction) King acknowledges the presence of an Other to counter evil. There is no *deus ex machina*, no rabbit pulled out of a hat at the end of the story to restore universal order. Instead, King plays it very carefully. In the first three-fourths of the novel, there are only a few enigmatic references to the "Turtle"; and when we finally encounter that entity, it is surprisingly static. It barely moves. The Turtle does not act to save the children; instead it answers questions and by doing so enables the children to save themselves. Yet it is clear that It and Turtle are of the same order of creation, so to speak, beyond humanity perhaps, but parallel to each other. In spite of It's pretensions to immortality, omniscience, and omnipresence, It is (again like Milton's Satan) no more than a secondary creation. In spite of It's overwhelming power in this world, and It's apparently commensurate (if not greater) power in the macrouniverse, It is only a creation. And the Turtle, we discover, is even more subject to the laws of time and mortality.

What makes *IT* different from anything else King has written, except perhaps "The Reach," is the intrusion of the Other into the struggle. Evil is powerful, but Good is not without its advocate. In the initial version of *The Stand*, for example, Randall Flagg seems almost to destroy himself; his precipitous actions confound his own plans. Some force for good may be involved, but we never perceive that force directly. In *IT*, the Other speaks—admittedly in King's down-home dialect but recognizably paralleling the Biblical "Behold my beloved son, in whom I am well pleased." The "son" is no deity, however, but a human who has opened himself to the promptings of the Other.

This additional layering of power helps keep *IT* from being merely an exploration of Lovecraftian horror or yet another variant on any of several folkloric patterns. Instead *IT* approaches the mythic, a sense that increases as the adult/children themselves draw closer to their final meeting with It. In describing that meeting, King almost ignores physical violence and force to allow the battle to take on a psychological, emotional, and spiritual nature.

In addition, King also resolves the long-standing conflict he has frequently delineated between the worlds of childhood and of adulthood. Initially *IT* suggests his earlier works. Children are victims, not only of monsters but of adults and of other children. George Denbrough dies violently in the opening pages, the precursor to literally hundreds of deaths implied or described. Many are at the hands of Pennywise the Clown; others result from the adult world as it impinges upon the child's. In some instances something even worse happens as, through their experiences with the adult world, children become insane, crippled spiritually until they become It's willing tool in destroying other children. Frequently, the deaths are graphic and chilling; to this extent, *IT* carries many of King's distinctive trademarks. But there are also essential differences.

First, many deaths do *not* occur. Pennywise and It's minions wonder what is happening. In spite of their best efforts, they are unable to destroy certain of their enemies; the seven, while undergoing physical and mental stress, seem unaccountably charmed.

And second, the seven achieve what few of King's characters even understood that they must strive for. They *blend* child and adult, building on the strengths inherent in each state. On one level, this seems an extension of the "sacrificial child" motif. Eddie figuratively marries his mother; mother and wife are archetypal Kingesque "monstrous women," a figure almost as pervasive in his fiction as the too-adult child. Beverly figuratively marries her father, a deeply disturbed, violent man unable to control his own desires as his daughter matures.

On another level, however, the blending gives *IT* unique power. The twenty-seven-year cycle of death roughly recapitulates a single generation. It's hope is that the seven, as adults, will be incapable of generating the force necessary to confront and destroy It. Mike Hanlon articulates the fears of all when he speculates on It's purpose behind the twenty-seven-year delay:

> And now, now that we no longer believe in Santa Claus, the Tooth Fairy, Hansel and Gretel, or the troll under the bridge, It is ready for us. *Come on back*, It says...*Come on back, and we'll see if you remember*

> the simplest thing of all: how it is to be children, se-
> cure in belief and thus afraid of the dark. (IT 894)

Later, King makes even more explicit the relationship between child-
like faith and the destruction of the monster. It realizes that the children had

> ...discovered an alarming secret that even It had not
> been aware of: that belief has a second edge. If there
> are ten thousand medieval peasants who create vam-
> pires by believing them real, there may be
> one—probably a child—who will imagine the stake
> necessary to kill it. But a stake is only stupid wood;
> the mind is the mallet which drives it home. (1017)

What actually occurs is that the characters must re-capture the
essence of childhood, an action symbolized by King's narrative structure. Moving with increasing frequency from 1958 to 1985 and back,
he does not complete either narrative independently. Instead, the adult
parallels the child in each of the seven (soon to be six) as they *remember* as adults at precisely the same pace they had *experienced* as children. In addition, they also return as much as possible to their physical
state as children. One gives up his contact lenses and resumes wearing
the thick glasses that made him the butt of so many jokes in grade
school; another begins to stutter again, his stutter increasing in intensity
as he approaches the core experience, by which time he becomes almost
nonverbal. To varying degrees, each recapitulates childhood—but with
a difference.

They become adult/children. They must recapture their innocence, their willingness to believe implicitly in what they know experi-
entially about Pennywise the Clown. The characters attempt to return
to that state of belief, bolstered this time by adult strength and perse-
verance.

King's attitudes toward sexuality demonstrate this merging of
the two worlds. Initially, again, there seems to be little change from
his earlier works. The first suggestions of sexuality focus on homosexuality; one of the first victims of the new cycle of terror is a gay man
set upon by straights, who throw him into the canal—and into the
waiting arms of It. As elsewhere, King's attitudes toward homosexuality are ambivalent. The theme occurs frequently in his fiction; it is often overtly negative as in "Children of the Corn" and the opening scene
of "Nona," but also frequently ambivalent, as in *The Long Walk*. In *IT*
the treatment of homosexuality becomes more openly vicious than ever.
Not only do the characters react negatively and strongly to the suggestion of homosexuality, but the narrative links (*i.e.*, the narrator's voice
itself) continue that harsh, stereotypic attitude. The gay man killed

never rises above the slickest of stereotypes, nor do reactions to his death ever overcome the hurdle of his sexual orientation.

King explains this orientation in terms of events during Bangor's sesquicentennial celebration, culminating in the death of a young asthmatic gay man thrown into the Kenduskeag Stream by three other young men and his subsequent death by asphyxiation. "I took notes on the police interrogation," King writes, and even though the official records were never used in court and were later destroyed, he says that

> ...a lot of the conversation in the chapter is reputedly what was said. It is, in fact, what I believe to be true. The ritual nature of the killing—at least when placed in the context of a summer festival—and the cross-connection to Eddie's asthma made it just too good to drop. So I used it to bookend George Denbrough's death. If the chapter strikes you as homophobic, please remember that this is a case of "We don't make the news, we just report it."[2]

In spite of these connections with external events, the novel does, however, focus on homosexuality as sub-theme. Much later in the narrative, even the hint of a homosexual relation is sufficient to drive one character into insanity; the text explicitly connects his subsequent actions with that single moment of crisis. Other elements in his family and background certainly moved him toward insanity, but King carefully notes that one action makes the insanity inevitable.

There is a certain justification for this attitude in the novel. By its nature, homosexuality opposes heterosexuality, the linking of man and woman in the deepest emotional bonds. And that intense bonding lies at the center of *IT*.

In earlier novels, sexuality had been almost invariably a threat to King's characters. Carrie dies because menstruation (and potential sexuality) triggers powers she is incapable of handling. The vampire in *'Salem's Lot* is a traditional image of threatening sexuality—particularly developed in the death of Susan Norton. The perverted sexuality of Nadine Cross and Harold Lauder in *The Stand* inhibits either of them from developing as mature adults; only the birth of a child to Frannie Goldsmith comes close to establishing a sense of sexuality as regenerative. Even in the early *The Long Walk*, sexuality is an overt threat; one of the boys risks death just to kiss and fondle a girl standing along the roadway. And in "The Raft," King carries this theme to its most fully developed ends. As Randy and LaVerne have intercourse on the raft, the blob-thing flows onto her hair and destroys her; his own shock, coupled with an emotional attachment, forces Randy into immobility—and condemns him as well. That story in fact becomes a symbol for the child afraid to engage the adult world directly. In spite of their surface pretensions to adulthood and sexuality, the four characters return to the raft too late in the year; they yearn for the simplicity of childhood that they simultaneously reject. King's revisions to the text in *Skeleton Crew* emphasize this image to the point that it becomes virtually impossible to miss.[4]

With *IT*, that negative emphasis changes. At first, of course, sexuality remains a mystery and a threat. Boys do not quite understand the mechanics of the sex act (also referred to as doing "it," with connections to the monster that are anything but accidental—sexuality is an unknown and potentially deadly monster for children). Girls understand a bit more but refuse to handle the realities other than through giggles and selfconscious embarrassment.

The It/it dichotomy develops most strongly in the passage where King finally allows his characters to move from childhood to adulthood. In a powerful scene, sexuality binds the seven—not the physical act of having sex but the emotional commitment of deeply binding and adult love. Sexuality becomes the key to survival, in a way that would have been impossible for almost any of King's earlier characters. The moment is handled as indirectly as possible; obviously the physical element of the act is critical, since those involved are eleven or twelve years old and none fully understands what it entails. Yet King continually emphasizes the *emotional* effects, not the physical. And in doing so, he transcends himself, to create a conclusion that is more positively emotionally stirring than anything else—again, with the possible exception of "The Reach."

In a recent letter discussing the novel, King wrote that *IT* culminates his treatment of children and monsters; he would not return to it again.[5] That is appropriate, since in *IT* his fictional children finally mature on their own, embracing the adult world consciously and willingly. They integrate the two levels of experience, and in doing so make possible the defeat of evil.

Put in those terms, *IT* sounds almost mythic. And it is. The conclusion is as powerful as cultural myth or archetype; the narrative is an extended rite of passage, with an externalized monster that represents (literally) the deepest fears of childhood that must be faced and overcome before the adult can develop into an independent and healthy individual. When I read King, I expect a strong ending. Rarely am I disappointed. In novel after novel, he adds just the right touch to confirm the narrative: *Pet Sematary* epitomizes the strength of his conclusions. The single word "Darling" chills the reader to the zero point. What I do not expect—and what *IT* gave me—is an intensely emotional awareness of the rightness of things, a quality that transcends fiction to touch upon the archetypal patterns we respond so deeply to. When I read such a novel (and they are rare), the power is so intense that words are inadequate—words, in fact, come between me and the experience.

This happened with *IT*. Although it has its share of crudities and harsh language, violence, and stylistic infelicities (including repetitions that may simply be inevitable in a novel, the manuscript for which is, as King put it, bigger than his own head), at the end, *IT* transcends itself, to stand as the most powerful novel King has yet written.

2. Stephen King's *IT*: The Transmutation of Genre

Stephen King is a consciously contemporary writer whose imagined worlds—no matter how deeply they descend into horror—are closely tied to the real world. Only rarely does he construct the medieval (or more usual, pseudo-medieval) worldview commonly associated with folklore. He is capable of such, as is evident in his creation of the threatened Kingdom of Delain in *The Eyes of the Dragon*, complete with castles, dragons, and evil magicians; in elements of The Territories in *The Talisman*; or in the castle episodes from *The Dark Tower*. More frequently, however, he simply chooses not to.

Instead, King's worlds are most often stridently contemporary. His characters drive Camaros and Volkswagon Beetles; they eat Big Macs and fries; they watch *An American Werewolf in London* in shopping-mall theaters; they wear Adidas running shoes and Oshkosh bib overalls. No matter how they might be connected to the supernatural horror—or horrors—that *also* populate King's imagination, his characters remain essentially modern and human.

Even at the level of horror, King generally eschews the more traditional folklore patterns, following instead recognizably literary sources. In *'Salem's Lot*, for example, his vampires have little to do with folkloric traditions defining the Undead. Instead, he draws heavily on Bram Stoker's *Dracula*, thus placing his tale at least two levels away from the original conventions. (The same technique occurs in Richard Kobritz's television adaptation of King's novel, in which the vampires alternately reflect Stoker's *Dracula* and F. W. Murnau's later film *Nosferatu*, itself a reflection of an alternate Eastern European tradition.)

Where his sources are not directly literary, they tend to be cinematic. The werewolf in *Cycle of the Werewolf* owes much to stereotypic Hollywood imagery, beginning with *The Wolf Man* in the 1930s and continuing to *An American Werewolf in London* (1981). In a sense, it is appropriate that the film version of King's text, with screenplay by King, return to the "classic" werewolf images of thirties' and forties' film, as opposed to the technologically innovative special effects of *An American Werewolf in London* or the self-parody of other films, particularly *Teen Wolf* (1985)—by so doing, King emphasizes his commitment to his sources. For King, cinema has become an acceptable variation on folklore and consequently a basic reservoir for images and themes.

25

Consequently, his "horrors" do not usually relate directly to traditional lore, especially to the oral traditions one associates with folklore. Instead, he works within contemporary forms as codified and defined by film and fantasy/horror literature. His monsters represent the modern world as it impinges upon the individual; as a result, they are frequently constructs of that modern world. In spite of the presence of vampires, werewolves, and ghosts in some of his fictions, most of King's truest (and most effective) horror lies in evocations of the unknown within the known.

For the society in which King lives and writes, one of the most pervasive images is the machine. From his earliest stories to his most recent novels, machines play central roles, replacing more traditional creatures from myth and legend. "The Mangler," for example, envisions an industrial ironing-machine ripping itself from concrete foundations and roaming the streets in search of blood; the subsequent film version unfortunately nearly ignores that image, replacing it with a rather flatly stereotypic suggestion of demon-worship. The haunted car in *Christine* is associated with ghostly presences, but the focus of the novel remains the car; quite appropriately, the film version of this story deletes the traditional ghosts entirely.

Similarly, in *The Tommyknockers* (1987), King consciously avoids evoking conventional monsters, working instead with machines and machine-presences as a means of critiquing the American obsession with gadgets. In the novel, the mechanical devices we surround ourselves with take on life and energy of their own. The results include a television set that "reveals" unsavory truths about neighbors, friends, and husband to an unstable woman named 'Becka Paulson, leading her into psychological terror, emotional upheaval, and physical death—all without any of the standard appurtenances of dark fantasy. Ambulatory, homicidal Coca-Cola machines and equally bloodthirsty little red wagons also figure prominently in *The Tommyknockers*, as do a variety of other machines.

When King does incorporate traditional elements into his fiction, however, they undergo radical transformations. Critics have noted traditional, folklore-oriented motifs in King's fictions, as in Alex E. Alexander's "Stephen King's Carrie: A Universal Fairy Tale"[6] and Chelsea Quinn Yarbro's "Cinderella's Revenge: Twists on Fairy Tale and Mythic Themes in the Work of Stephen King."[7] Certainly those elements are present in King, yet he often consciously mutes them, subordinates them to literary and cinematic influences more germane to mainstream, twentieth-century American culture and consequently less intimately connected with folk traditions, as is most evident in *IT*.

In progress for almost eight years, the novel represents, in King's words, "a final summing up of everything I've tried to say in the last twelve years on the two central subjects of my fiction: monsters and children."[8] Stefan Kanfer emphasizes the contemporary, cinematic qualities of the novel when he writes:

> Before he began the book, Stephen thought about a favorite image: the entire cast of the Bugs Bunny show coming on at the beginning, Yosemite Sam, Bugs Bunny, Daffy Duck, and the gang. In a surge of adolescent enthusiasm, King burbled, "Wouldn't it be great to bring on all the monsters one last time? Bring them all on—*Dracula*, *Frankenstein*, *Jaws*, The Werewolf, *The Crawling Eye*, *Rodan*, *It Came From Outer Space*, and call it *It*." But how could he combine them all in one book? Simple. Use a Tulpa—the Tibetan word for a creature created by the mind.[9]

Even more germane to this discussion, however, King has defined the genesis of the novel in terms of folktales; one day, while he was living in Colorado and engaged in writing *The Stand*, he walked across a wooden bridge:

> I was wearing boots, and I could hear the heels clocking hollowly on the wood. I suppose I should have thought of Randy Flagg, since I was all wrapped up in his life just then, but instead I thought of the story of Billy Goats Gruff, the troll who says "Who's that trip-trapping on my bridge?" and the whole story just bounced into my mind on a pogo-stick. Not the characters, but the split time-frame, the accelerating bounces that would end with a complete breakdown which might result in a feeling of "no-time," all the monsters that were one monster...the troll under the bridge, of course, *It*.[10]

These passages suggest that *IT* enjoys closer affinities with traditional motifs than most of King's works. The desire to re-create a sense of "no-time" parallels the time-in-timelessness effect of the conventional, formulaic "Once upon a time" openings so common in fairy tales. As is usual with King, however, he transforms that incantatory opening into something that at once partakes of the effect of the original and moves into the idiom of contemporary society from the first paragraph of the novel:

> The terror which would not end for another twenty-eight years—if it ever did end—began, so far as I know or can tell, with a boat made from a sheet

of newspaper floating down a gutter swollen with
rain. (1)

Internal references to older tales also connect *IT* with traditional
sources, suggesting the power that such narratives hold:

> As if in a dream [Bill] heard Miss Davies, the
> assistant librarian, reading to the little ones: *Who is
> that trip-trapping on my bridge?* And he saw them,
> the little ones, the babies, leaning forward, their faces
> still and solemn, their eyes reflecting the eternal fasci-
> nation of the fairy-story: would the monster be bested
> or would It feed? (864)

King expands his "family" of goats to seven, defined within
the text as a magical, mystical number, then doubles it as he works with
those characters as children and as adults. He also incorporates nu-
merological significance into the novel when he sets the two major sequences of actions in 1958 and 1985. In addition to a simple Orwellian
reversal (after all, *Nineteen Eighty-Four* was written in 1948), King's
dates define a span of twenty-seven years between the outbreaks of terror—three times three times three, emphasizing again the magical values of numbers, particularly three, in folk materials.

Even more significantly, the text itself refers overtly to traditions, folk tales, and legends from several cultures: the Golem (1022),
Hansel and Gretel (894), Santa Claus (894), the Gingerbread Man
(731), the werewolf and vampire (including concomitant legends of the
efficacy of silver bullets and crucifixes in destroying them), the
mummy, and others. As King suggests early in the novel when one of
his characters descends into a dank cellar,

> Smells of dirt and wet and long-gone vegetables
> would merge into one unmistakable ineluctable smell,
> the smell of the monster, the apotheosis of all mon-
> sters. (6-7)

Briefly, the plot of *IT* encompasses the attempts of seven children (and their adult selves twenty-seven years later) to defeat a creature
that has existed for generations beneath the streets of Derry, Maine.
The creature is always a threat, but its depredations increase in intensity
according to an unvarying rhythm, cresting every twenty-seven years
with a year-long cycle of death. It feeds on human flesh, to be sure;
but more importantly, like a psychic vampire, It is nourished by fear
and terror as well. To insure a full measure of both, It manifests itself
to It's victims, changing its outward form to match their imaginations.
Each of the seven children sees an entirely different "creature," and

each creature touches a deep psychological chord in the individual child. King refers to the protean monster as "Pennywise the Clown," as much for simplicity's sake as because that manifestation is the first detailed in the novel; later It appears as a werewolf, as the walking dead, as parasitic insect-things, and as a giant spider-entity, among other forms.

The characters' primary quest, both as children and as adults, is to discover the nature of the creature and the means by which It might be defeated. As children, they wound It severely; as adults, they gather again in Derry to confront It in It's recovered strength and attempt It's destruction.

As with so many quest tales, knowledge is the key to everything. King carefully orchestrates the narrative so that the readers discover only as much about the creature as the characters know; and their knowledge, in turn, must balance between what they experience as children and the memories that they gradually reconstruct as adults.

The novel is unusually long, even for King, who admits to occasional "literary elephantiasis"; the text runs 1138 pages. Over half of the narrative elapses before the characters—and consequently the readers—begin to understand the nature of the creature they must battle. By that time, It has appeared as a vampire, a werewolf, a clown, and an amorphous monster-thing that gushes blood from sinks and drains. To this point, the novel seems essentially a compendium of horror motifs, an indulgence in monsters.

In truth, however, It is none of the forms It has assumed—or better said, It contains all of them and more. It is a *glamour*,

> the Gaelic name for the creature which was haunting Derry; other races and other cultures at other times had different words for it, but they all meant the same thing. The Plains Indians called it a manitou, which sometimes took the shape of a mountain-lion or an elk or an eagle.... The Himalayans called it a *tallus* or *tælus*, which meant an evil magic being that could read your mind and then assume the shape of the thing you were most afraid of. In central Europe it had been called *eylak*, brother of the *vurderlak*, or vampire. In France it was *le loup-garou*, or skin-changer, a concept that had been crudely translated as the Werewolf.... [It] could be anything, anything at all: a wolf, a hawk, a sheep, even a bug. (674-75; see also 1015-1016)

Understanding the nature of the adversary leads the children to a possible advantage—the Himalayans had developed a ritual to expel the monster. The children attempt the ritual and are partially successful; as adults they must recreate the innocence and unquestioning belief of children and re-attempt the ritual. To fail this time means their deaths and the continuation of It forever.

At this point in *IT*, King seems to have reversed his usual pattern. Instead of drawing exclusively on literary or cinematic models, he begins with the monsters of literature and film (Michael Landon as the teenage werewolf, for example), then explains the many manifestations of It in terms of original folk materials. The monster is *not* a construct of the twentieth century; quite to the contrary, It has existed over the generations, has touched many cultures and left Its mark on them. For once, King seems to argue that the aboriginal tales of shape-shifters have more power than their modern counterparts as codified and defined in books and films.

That is itself an illusion, however, as so much in *IT* is revealed as illusion. Bill is correct in identifying It as glamour, manitou, eylak, tallus, or loup-garou; It is each of those in different societies. But merely giving It a name (or multiplicity of names) does not identify It's essence.

And for that, King cannot fall back on the traditions of folk lore. As always in his prose, the stark traditions are not sufficient; they do not speak directly enough to the audience he addresses.

In fact, King is forced between two alternatives, structural decisions defined by Tzvetan Todorov in his analysis of the fantastic in literature. King has established the "reality" of the creature by referring to myth, legend and folklore; that in turn demands that the characters, and the readers, hesitate between two alternatives. The creatures of myth might in fact have been actual, in which case the novel ceases to be dark fantasy and becomes a skewed sort of science fiction, on the order of Whitley Strieber's *The Wolfen* (1978) with its alternate-evolution werewolves, and *The Hunger* (1980), with its similarly "authenticated" vampires; or Dean Koontz's *Strangers* (1986), which moves (as does *IT*) from horror into science fiction. Or, as a second option, the mythic underpinnings themselves might remain in the realm of the supernatural, and both the characters and the readers must accept the intrusion of the irrational into our universe; the novel remains an exercise in supernatural horror.

In the final chapters of *IT*, King makes his decision and re-defines the creature. Having begun as a representative of literary and cinematic monsters, subsequently transformed into a creature central to legends and tales from several cultures, It ultimately transmutes into the archetypal "creature" of the twentieth-century. In a blend of H. P. Lovecraft and contemporary science fiction, King reveals that It—and thus all of the legendary and mythic entities It represents—is in fact an alien, stranded on this planet long before the rise of human civilization.

King thus once more alters subtly the generic expectations of the novel—the "reading protocols" readers must apply to the text, to borrow Samuel R. Delany's phrase. We have moved from horror/dark-fantasy to folklore and myth; we now move again into science fiction, with the assertion of alien presences that account not only for the narrative we have before us but for the entire panoply of myth, legend, and lore that has accumulated around the shape-shifters of all cultures.

By doing so, King initiates almost immediately another and more crucial generic transmutation. We no sooner become aware of It as a Lovecraftian "Great Old One," as a stranded alien divorced from the moral, ethical, and spiritual norms of the human race (and for whom children simply represent the best possible source of nourishment for a pregnant creature), than we immediately transcend that entity to encounter another—the Turtle.

The Turtle is a difficult figure in *IT*. King mentions it early in the novel (as early as page 8, in fact), but in a work as long as *IT*, such foreshadowings tend to become lost. When the Turtle finally appears, it is in what amounts to a dream-vision, an out-of-body experience that breaks through the generic barriers of science fiction and approaches myth itself. Certainly the Turtle has sufficient analogues in mythology, particularly in the image of the great turtle swimming through the oceans of the universe, supporting on its back the four elephants which in turn support the world itself.

Even more critically, the Turtle reveals that something else exists beyond the limits and powers of It *and* the Turtle. The monster which is Pennywise the Clown may be an alien from another dimension struggling to gain sufficient power to return. And the Turtle may suggest supernal wisdom, age, and strength inherent in the universe; as it says, "I made the universe, but please don't blame me for it; I had a bellyache" (1053). But when the children-become-adults seek It's ultimate destruction, they discover that the Turtle has died. In its place they find... Something else, a power beyond comprehension and defying understanding. The Something speaks—telepathically, perhaps, or spirit to spirit—in a New England parody of the Biblical "Behold my beloved son, in whom I am well pleased":

And clearly, [Bill] heard the Voice of the Other;
the Turtle might be dead, but whatever had invested it
was not.
"Son, you did real good." (1094)

Working through folklore, horror, the literature and film of dark fantasy, and science fiction, King arrives at full circle, replacing centuries-old variations on myth with Myth itself. For the first time in King's fictions, evil is not only destroyed, but his characters confront the Numinous directly, experience a spiritual meaning within the universe that defies their (and our) expectations.

As a result, the conclusion of *IT* touches on levels King has not attained before, convincing emotionally as well as intellectually.

In part, the power of the conclusion lies in the groundwork King has prepared; and much of that groundwork incorporates his careful weaving of legend and lore into the novel itself. Pennywise the Clown is among King's most potent monsters precisely because It is, as King envisioned, "the apotheosis of all monsters." As It draws the power of many traditions, of nightmares and terrors on many levels, and spreads that power incrementally throughout the text, It lays the groundwork not only for It's own destruction, but for the apprehension of the Other. Without the horror of first—the monster—the sublimity of the second would not have been possible.

II.

STEPHEN KING, SCIENCE FICTION, AND *THE TOMMYKNOCKERS*[1]

During the last few months of 1987, one of the most talked-about issues among King's readers was his announced "retirement." Coupled with the projected demise of *Castle Rock* a year later, with the December 1988 issue, the few published statements about King's immediate and future plans caused ripples of concern among his fans—Was it true? Would there be no more novels from Stephen King?

In actual practice, what occurred was less a "retirement" than a change. King's writings took a distinctly different direction, the first of several such disjunctures in King's career over the past decade years, each dealing primarily with a conscious shift in content while maintaining narrative continuity through storytelling style and recurrent motifs, as in the Dark Tower elements in *Insomnia*. The sense of changing directions was implicit in *IT*, with its farewell to monsters and children under threat; it continued in *Misery* and *The Tommyknockers*; and it ultimately culminated in *Needful Things*, with the literal destruction of Castle Rock and the implication that wherever King's fictions might take him, he was finished exploring the haunted environments around that town. In a more recent and perhaps less obvious paradigm shift, King seemed almost to be entering the "establishment mainstream," with overtly socially conscious novels such as *Gerald's Game*, and, to a lesser extent, *Dolores Claiborne* and *Rose Madder*.

Stephanie Leonard's clarification of King's intentions in the September 1987 *Castle Rock* put the issue into perspective: "Stephen King is not really retiring.... He is hoping to cut back on work.... There will not be any more five-book years any time soon; he does plan to continue writing and to publish less."[2] And, in fact, King concentrated on several one-book years, leading up to what promises to be another record-breaking explosion in 1996-1997, with the six-part serialized novel, *The Green Mile*, beginning in March, 1996; Stephen King's *Desperation* and Richard Bachman's *The Regulators*, both published in July/August of 1996; and the promise of new installments of The Dark Tower series shortly thereafter.

The misunderstanding concerning King's writing plans laid to rest, however, there still remained an odd sense of closure as King, his readers, and even the newsletter that bore his name approached the end of 1987 and the publication of *The Tommyknockers*. Even though the novel did not represent King's "swan song," even though there was clearly the promise of more—including the unexpurgated version of *The Stand*, several short stories, and continued work on *The Dark Tower* (completion of which is, as noted above, promised for sometime around 1997-1998)—*The Tommyknockers* was nonetheless a terminal piece in a number of ways.

As early as 1986, King referred to *The Tommyknockers* as representing an end of sorts in his career. In a letter accompanying a manuscript copy of *IT* in March, 1986, King noted that *IT* was the last monster-oriented novel he was working on. *Misery*, he wrote, was not a monster-novel at all; its horrors were tied to the world around us, and therefore, for many readers, the novel was even more fundamentally frightening than anticipated when it appeared in 1987. In *The Tommyknockers*, he added, any true "monsters" had already been dead for millions of years, and their influence was residual rather than immediate and physical.[3]

In addition, the letter discussed at length the resolution of one of King's most persistent themes, the threatened child. Overtly and consciously supplanted in several recent novels by the parallel theme of the threatened/abused woman, most notably in *Gerald's Game*, *Dolores Claiborne*, and *Rose Madder*,[4] King's child-at-risk had served him admirably through such now-classic books as *The Shining*, *The Dead Zone*, *Pet Sematary*, and, to a lesser extent, *Christine*. In their own way, even the earliest Bachman books had concentrated heavily on children/adolescents, as in *Rage* and *The Long Walk*. But by the time *IT* was completed, King was preparing to mark "closed" to that part of his career. In *IT*, children not only survive an immediate threat but make the difficult transition from childhood to adulthood, from incipient sexuality to responsible sexuality, and finally to potential parenthood. He would not, he stated in the letter, concentrate on children in danger in forthcoming novels.

With its exclusively and almost stridently adult characters, *Misery* confirmed that comment; *The Tommyknockers* similarly continued the sense that one of King's heretofore perennial concerns had, in fact, been laid to rest. The key actors are adults: Jim Gardener, Bobbi Anderson, Ruth McCausland, Ev Hillman, and the adult population of Haven. Child-figures are less central in the novel, often more important through their absence than their presence, even though children, most notably Hilly and David Brown, do appear and do stimulate actions by Jim Gardener and Ev Hillman that lead to the defeat of the Tommyknockers. In addition, several characters are obsessed by traumatic incidents in their childhoods—a motif that become increasingly potent in later novels, including *Gerald's Game*, *Dolores Claiborne*, and *The Green Mile*.

Thus, instead of concentrating on the threatened child, *The Tommyknockers* is essentially about the threatened adult, the grown-up locked within a world that is as dangerous and as unsure as the children's worlds King delineated in *Carrie, The Shining, Christine*, "The Raft," and other stories. More critically, it is a world on the verge of destroying itself through the actions of other putative adults, over whom King's characters have little or no influence or control; it is a world "out of control...Has been since...oh, around 1939....We reached critical mass along about 1965. It's out of control. The explosion will come soon" (110). Even drunk, Jim Gardener tenuously balances hope and despair when he considers that

> it was possible—unlikely but possible—that he might
> write a few more good poems before the madmen who
> had stuffed a shotgun up the asshole of the world de-
> cided to pull the trigger. (61)

In several places, Gardener notes that the Nuclear Clock (indicating how close humanity is to mass destruction) is now set at two minutes before midnight. Yet even in light of the perilous condition of the world, and of his own obsession with pending nuclear disaster, Gardener nevertheless struggles to the death to save what little remains of goodness he sees around him, particularly in Bobbi Anderson. His responses move from self-centered and psychologically juvenile acts, symbolized by his drunkenness, to responsible and committed adult acts, acts of community rather than individuality, as the isolated poet-artist becomes intimately involved with the fate of Haven, Maine. As King has aged and matured, so have his characters, and *The Tommyknockers* represents a key step toward the logical outcome of that process.

For these reasons, then, re-reading *The Tommyknockers* almost a decade after it first appeared does suggest, if not an ending, at least a distinct angling in a new direction.

At the same time, the novel expands on secondary themes initiated in such novels as *The Stand* and *IT*. *The Tommyknockers* experiments with the differing purposes and assumptions of science fiction and horror as literary genres. To a degree, *The Stand* (more prominently perhaps in the original edition but still readily apparent in the "complete and uncut edition") opens in what seems a science-fictional world, the world of a technological development escaped from human control and threatening humanity...the Super Flu. Then gradually, as characters begin to dream, to intuit the presence of good and evil forces, and to embark on fantasy-epic quests, the novel shifts subtly to dark fantasy, with more than its share of specifically horrific elements.[5]

IT demonstrates an inverse movement: a novel that begins by asserting horror-fantasy concludes with a Lovecraftian science-fictional

35

ending as aliens from space supplant more traditional monsters. Given that *IT* shows Lovecraftian influences throughout, however, it is not surprising that in fact the differentiation between the two kinds of antagonists—aliens and monsters—remains marginal or that a number of readers and critics were dissatisfied with the abrupt assertion of a spider-alien from space as a resolution to the novel.

More recently, King further developed his interest in the intersection of genres (what Dean Koontz has called "cross-genre fiction") in *Rose Madder*, which begins as an essentially mainstream novel focusing on physical and mental abuse, then gradually invites readers into a world of mythic fantasy closely and imagistically allied with horror. And in an even more complex interplay of literary forms, the novels exploring the Dark Tower mythos (including *The Stand*, *The Eyes of the Dragon*, and *Insomnia*, as well as the Dark Tower episodes themselves) shift adroitly between science fiction and fantasy, epic and horror, myth and the western, action-adventure and romance, easily categorizing themselves as among King's most ambitious and complicated explorations of literary genres and their limits.

The Tommyknockers, however, seems almost immediately to thrust readers into an explicitly science-fictional context, with the discovery of an alien spacecraft. Only as the novel progresses do we discover, along with King's characters, that this fundamentally SF context has been continuously subverted and transformed into quintessential horror in ways surpassing even the transitions in *The Stand*.

Before that awareness becomes full-blown, however, readers are treated to a number of seemingly incidental elements in *The Tommyknockers*, not the least being King's self-reflexive references to himself and to his previous stories. If King had in fact been planning to "retire," *The Tommyknockers* would have represented a perfect farewell, if only because it frequently alludes to scenes, situations, characters, and images already familiar to his readers. When Jim Gardener wakes up on a deserted beach after a week-long drunk, he is interrupted in his contemplation of suicide by a kid in a T-shirt blowing off fourth-of-July firecrackers—an unusually insightful boy whose words rapidly take on the weight of omens. Because of the subtleties of King's handling of the chance meeting, it is no surprise to discover that Jim Gardener, itinerant poet and sometime alcoholic, has slept insensate on Arcadia Beach, that the old hotel *looming* in the distance (in the Melvillian sense of the word, an echo of King's earlier reference to *Moby Dick* [70] and adumbration of a more extended discussion of "Ishmael the Sailor-Man" [130-131]) is the Alhambra, and that the boy's name is Jack (90-91). For an instant, a crack opens in *The Tommyknockers*, and the mythic power that King and Straub invested in *The Talisman* floods through, transcending the spare narrative lines and infusing the boy's words (and King's) with true "omenish" power.

This kind of fragmentary, momentary cross-fertilization is fairly common in King's novels. Occasionally, as in *The Stand*, *The Dark Tower* segments, *The Eyes of the Dragon*, and *Insomnia*—with their intricate intertwining of Randall Flagg and other RFs with half-perceived visions of the Dark Tower—the technique suggests that King's novels are not entirely independent but instead overlap considerably more than a casual reading might indicate. The suggestion was further validated in *Gerald's Game* and *Dolores Claiborne*, in both of which climactic events take place during the same eclipse—deeds of darkness done in darkness. Lest casual readers miss the connection, the two books contain obviously similar double-page woodcut illustrations on the title pages and identical maps outlining the path of the eclipse on July 20, 1963.

In *The Tommyknockers*, such reflexive allusions build until the novel becomes a skeletal compendium of King's previous stories. Specific incidents recall moments from *IT*, as when a mutating Havenite drives through Derry in search of batteries:

> Tommy had begun to hallucinate; as he drove up Wentworth Street, he thought he saw a clown grinning up at him from an open sewer manhole—a clown with shiny silver dollars for eyes and a clenched white glove filled with balloons. (378)

Earlier, less specific references to *IT* suggest a dark undercurrent in *The Tommyknockers*. Gardener hesitates to look into the shed window, fearing that he might see a "white face" with a "mouthful of filed cannibal teeth," an echo of one of Pennywise's disguises, followed by a Haven-toolshed version of "We all float down here" (161); Sister Anne's teeth similarly not only suggest James Bond's nemesis but even more directly Pennywise's teeth (396). Ruth McCausland is specifically described as a childless librarian (214) and the heart and soul of Haven, paralleling Mike Hanlon's role in *IT*. Ev Hillman, representing Haven in exile, lies in his dark hotel room in Derry and listens to "chuckling noises coming from the drains" (277); he thinks that the sounds prove he is going crazy, but readers of *IT* could easily suggest another explanation. And, while not reflecting King's artistic purposes in *The Tommyknockers*, in an oddly appropriate addition to the film version, the script tacitly acknowledged *The Tommyknockers*'s tonal affinity to *IT* by including a threatening clown doll among the half dozen that attack Ruth McCausland.

The Dead Zone appears allusively when Gardener contemplates suicide—jumping into the "dead zone," as he calls it (88). Later, however, Ev Hillman makes explicit connections between what is happening in Haven and the stories he has heard of a John Smith, who taught for a time in Cleaves Mills and who had demonstrated certain psychic powers

(277). Still later, a journalist named David Bright appears, at first briefly, as if he were just another brief allusion to *The Dead Zone* (and beyond that to King's experiences working on *The Maine Campus*, his college newspaper, edited by David Bright). By the end of *The Tommyknockers*, however, Bright has become an important secondary character, a particularly stable character in an increasingly unstable situation. As the situation near Haven reaches its climax, Bright remembers "poor, damned Johnny Smith, who had sometimes touched objects and gotten 'feelings' about them" (486). Again and again, the force of *The Dead Zone* filters through *The Tommyknockers*, an invisible presence never quite intruding into the text but constantly underlying it—and to that extent paralleling the effects of the alien space ship on the world of Bobbi Anderson and Jim Gardener.

When the government finally stumbles on to what is happening in Haven, Maine, and decides that it must take immediate action, it is no coincidence that one character identifies himself as associated, not with the FBI or the CIA, but with "the Shop." Earlier, Bobbi Anderson had expressed fears that her discovery would be taken over by authoritarian figures from "the NSA or the Shop" (157). And, lest the reader miss the connection with *Firestarter*, King's narrator notes that the Shop's installation in Virginia was once "burned to the ground by a child" (556).

The process continues with less direct but nonetheless recognizable references to *Silver Bullet* ("My beer is Rheingold the dry beer"); to *The Stand* and Arnette, Texas (501); to *Thinner* and the threat of uncontrolled weight loss; to *Pet Sematary* and the threatened death of a child beneath the wheels of a speeding delivery truck (186); to *Cujo* and attacks by crazed, vicious dogs (215); to *Roadwork* and death by brain tumor (214); and to *'Salem's Lot*, vampires (psychic rather than physical), and the abdication of responsibility by public officials.

On a lesser scale, *The Tommyknockers* suggests fragments of short stories as well. Certainly no reader familiar with King's short fiction will miss the much-revised version of "The Revelations of 'Becka Paulson," which originally appeared in *Rolling Stone* in 1984. The Big Injun Woods fire is described in terms reminiscent of "The Mangler," as the conflagration approaches with a roar, "as if the world's biggest open-hearth furnace had sprouted legs and was slowly approaching..."(495). There are also echoes of "The Revenge of Lardass Hogan" and its cataclysmic pie-eating contest (524); of "The Ballad of the Flexible Bullet," with its literary-minded fornits; of "Big Wheels: A Tale of the Laundry Game"; and of "Dolan's Cadillac," which by the time *The Tommyknockers* appeared had only appeared in the pages of *Castle Rock*.

Even films made from King's novels surface momentarily, as Gard conjures an image of himself entering the Tommyknockers's "New and Improved Workshop" with an axe, a Jack Nicholson leer, and a manic *"Heeeeeere's GARDENER!"* (420), an image from *The Shining*. And the motile homicidal Coke machine and other assorted gadgets guarding Haven seem to reflect King's earlier conception of murderous machinery in *Maximum Overdrive*.

If *IT* represented a compendium of horror motifs, rummaging widely through the traditional stock of monsters, creatures, and boogeymen, then *The Tommyknockers* represents almost a compendium to Stephen King himself—a fond farewell, as it were, to the tales of the past before turning himself in new directions (the process of bidding farewell would continue for several years, through the burning of Castle Rock in *Needful Things*, that allowed King to deal not only with adult-related horrors but also with much wider physical landscapes, as in *Insomnia, Rose Madder*, and *The Green Mile*).

But King does not allow the allusive process to become mindlessly self-congratulatory. In fact the single overt reference *to* Stephen King puts him and his work clearly into a perspective—even if it seems a mistaken perspective for most readers. Midway through the novel, Ev Hillman compares Bobbi Anderson's westerns with novels "all full of make-believe monsters and a bunch of dirty words, like the ones that fellow who lived up in Bangor wrote." In comparison, he concludes, hers are "Goddam good westerns" (287).

Earlier in the story, King even answers one of the criticisms leveled against his writing. One reader had pointed to a line in a King story, ostensibly "hissed" by the speaker, and noted that since there were no sibilants in the words in question, it would be impossible to "hiss" them. Apparently King was aware of that linguistic problem, since one of the least appealing characters in *The Tommyknockers* "hisses" the line "Quit it, Gardener." King follows the line with a note of explanation: "There were no sibilants in the words she spoke, making a hiss an impossibility, but she hissed just the same" (79). Criticism duly noted, registered, and answered.

As Hillman's comments about that Bangor writer suggest, amplified by King's self-reflexive incursion into language and sound, *The Tommyknockers* is (like *Misery* and the subsequent components of a "writer's trilogy," "Secret Window, Secret Garden" from *Four Past Midnight*, and *The Dark Half*) in part concerned with the art and craft of writing. Gardener's poetry, stalled in its development but potentially powerful, becomes a metaphor for Gardener's own erratic responses to life, while Bobbi Anderson's decision to write westerns becomes a pivotal moment in her life, an episode that makes her what she is and prepares her for the experiences that the discovery of the alien ship brings.

Specifically, though, the novel is about writing science fiction and horror, about the genres themselves, and about the connections between them. King refers to several contemporary SF writers, particularly Philip K. Dick and Poul Anderson. Hugo Gernsback, the putative "founding father" of modern science fiction, makes a brief cameo appearance as well. But, lest it seem that science fiction has an exclusive influence on *The Tommyknockers*, King also alludes to horror writers. H. P. Lovecraft's "The Colour Out of Space" provides a structural framework for much of the narrative in *The Tommyknockers*. In Lovecraft's story, an alien artifact plummets to earth, resulting in, among other things, a garden that is spectacularly productive, but the vegetables that grow there are monstrous inside and ultimately inedible—precisely what happens in Bobbi Anderson's garden. Lovecraft's signature vocabulary also surfaces in *The Tommyknockers*, with references to "eldritch" and "rugose." Edgar Allan Poe is suggested by the new and Improved bells of the Haven church: "the bells, the bells, the calling of the bells" (301). And perhaps coincidentally, a section on the same page, beginning with "The calling of the bells," deals with a seductive young woman named Annabelle. Several chapters later, Gardener himself quotes from "The Tell-Tale Heart," even crediting Poe with the line (353). The text also cites Peter Straub and *Floating Dragon*, a novel that not only completes a triptych including *The Talisman* and *IT*, but that also has strong and definite thematic relations to *The Tommyknockers*.

Even more importantly, perhaps, *The Tommyknockers* draws heavily on the visual imagery of science-fiction and horror films—and especially those films of the fifties that King has referred to so often as influencing his imagination. In *Danse Macabre*, King differentiates between two sorts of fifties' films: "*The Day the Earth Stood Still* is one of a select handful—the real science fiction movies. The ancient saucerians of *Earth vs. the Flying Saucers*, on the other hand, are emissaries of a much more common breed of film, the horror-show."6 In *The Tommyknockers*, King makes it explicit that he is *not* writing science fiction as such. His earlier attempts at doing so, including "The Jaunt" and "Beachworld," both from *Skeleton Crew*, had demonstrated that even his overt science-fiction stories were so only on the surface; their substrata remain unapologetically horror. In *The Tommyknockers*, King does not even allow that surface sense to endure unaltered. In spite of the aliens-from-space theme, in spite of the carry-over from *IT*'s alien spider-entity, in spite of the fact that the original Tommyknockers were in some senses "little green men" (a touch that simultaneously acknowledges and parodies the most obvious conventions of science fiction story-telling), in spite of the uses and abuses of technology that provide a sub-text to *The Tommyknockers*—in spite of these connections, King is adamant that this novel is *not* science fiction. When both Bobbi Anderson and Jim Gardener first touch the thing Bobbi Anderson has partially excavated, they identify it almost instinctively as a "flying saucer." It is *not* an "alien spacecraft," they realize, not an interstellar vessel, not any of the things science-fiction writers might imagine—nor should it be graced with such high-toned labels. It is simply a flying saucer: "No self-respecting science fiction writer would put one in his story, and no self-respecting editor would touch it with a ten-foot pole," Gardener thinks, connecting the term with the excesses of tabloid journalism and religious eccentricity (144). Virtually no one in the novel refers to the artifact as a spacecraft, at least not for the first two-thirds of the text; it is undeniably a flying saucer, a thing of horror and fear.

And the term is frighteningly accurate. *The Tommyknockers* is about a flying saucer, not an interstellar vessel or even an alien spacecraft. This vehicle is "the oldest haunted house in the universe" (545) and it cradles monsters, not aliens. The Tommyknockers were certainly from another world and had contacted many worlds before dying on Earth; but they are, in the deepest sense, *monsters* rather than *aliens*. They are like the Krell, or even better, like the creature from the Id that the Krell unleashed upon themselves in the classic film *Forbidden Planet*—technologically advanced but morally bankrupt (and the novel makes much use of Altair-4 and its monsters, even mentioning "Robby the Robot and Dr. Morbius" [319]). The Tommyknockers are monsters whose greed and cruelty destroyed their own lives and now threaten (and ultimately destroy) the lives of nearly everyone in and around Haven. The novel also refers to Howard Hawks's 1951 film *The Thing*, as well as to *The Day of the Triffids*—in short, to that now-classic sub-genre of black-and-white films that concentrated on the horror of alien invasion and on the horror of revealing what, at the deepest levels, humanity is capable of.

That is what *The Tommyknockers* emphasizes. Although King includes a spacecraft and aliens and mattermission and alternate worlds; although he alludes to *Firestarter*, which is occasionally classified as science rather than as horror on the basis of his inclusion of mind-altering drugs; although *The Tommyknockers* talks at length about the problems of nuclear proliferation and nuclear pollution, of governments stripping freedom and choice from their peoples, of the energy crisis, and of the innumerable other problems confronting the contemporary world—although all of these are essential parts of the novel, *The Tommyknockers* is still fundamentally about horror.

King asserts a propulsive force for his flying saucer, but he never tries to explain it other than through the gruesome images associated with chained and dead galley slaves and mysterious psychic vampirism. The mechanics of space travel seem alien to his interests, and instead he relies on what is essentially magic clothed as science. He asserts that the people of Haven are *becoming* Tommyknockers; he never explains precisely why. And any questions as to how human physiology can alter and mutate to become alien physiology, even to apparently including a different base chemical than carbon, are not only left unanswered, but are almost unasked. He *describes* the physical and psychological changes they undergo, but he shows little if any interest in *how* those changes occur. He works superficially with the most readily recognizable elements of science fiction; he does not, however, concern himself with the essential extrapolations from current technology, or with the speculations on possibility and probability that characterize contemporary science fiction.

Instead, in spite of its alien spacecraft and its remnants of alien intelligence and personality, *The Tommyknockers* more closely resembles *The Cycle of the Werewolf* than a science-fictional tale by H. G. Wells or Jules Verne or Philip K. Dick or Poul Anderson. In *Cycle*, there is no reason why a werewolf should appear in Tarker's Mill; King simply asserts that "its time is now, its place is here." Similarly, there is no reason why Bobbi Anderson should stumble on an outcropping of metal and begin an inevitable process of destruction. She simply does. It is time for it. The first lines of the novel assert the inevitability of events: "Anderson literally stumbled over her destiny....That stumble was the root of the matter; all the rest was nothing but history" (11). In a world two minutes from Nuclear Midnight—and already well into what Koontz has characterized in novels such as *Dragon Tears* as the pre-millennial cotillion—it is time to confront the technological and social horrors we have created and to realize that there are horrors even worse.

This is what makes *The Tommyknockers* an intriguing and ultimately a satisfying novel. It does not cross genres, in spite of the surface trappings of science fiction. It remains true to the roots of King's imagination in spite of the sense that it does conclude a phase in his writing career. It concentrates on what King does best: portraying essentially good people in extraordinary situations that bring out not only the goodness and strength in each of them, but also the ambiguity and the darkness. There are, as well, essentially evil characters, especially sister Anne, perhaps the least effective character in the novel, an extreme (almost unbelievably extreme) version of earlier "monstrous women" including Margaret White from *Carrie*, Mrs. Carmody from "The Mist," and *Misery*'s own Annie Wilkes.[7] The darkness is rarely that confined, rarely that limited, however; and part of the power of *The Tommyknockers* lies in King's recognition that light and dark coexist, even in the best of characters (another thematic connection to *The Stand* and *IT* made explicit in the concluding pages of *Needful Things*).

In *The Tommyknockers*, the darkness is allowed to grow. The strongest characters weaken, succumb to the evil, even die; but in their struggles and their sacrifices, there is something of the light, something of the strength that allows others to carry on and ultimately defeat the Tommyknockers. Even in death, those who have loved influence the living.

After the positive ending of *IT*, after the restoration at the end of *Misery*, the conclusion of *The Tommyknockers* seems bleak. All but two of the major characters are dead—and those two are children who do not fully understand what has happened to them. Even so, the novel avoids the unalleviated, horrifying darkness implicit in the final words of *Pet Sematary*. There has been change, fear, hatred, even death. In some cases, there has been violent and explicitly gruesome and deeply disturbing death. But there has also been growth through pain into strength. If there is a world beyond this one—not a science-fictional world one might reach in a flying saucer, but a spiritual one, from which the dead can speak to the living, as the novel suggests in its final pages—that growth has meaning.

The Tommyknockers did not signal King's "retirement." The ambitiousness, for example, of a ground-breaking serialized novel, *The Green Mile* appearing in the same year has seen Stephen King publishing *Desperation* and "RICHARD BACHMAN" publishing *The Regulators*, with the promise of the fourth Dark Tower novel, *Wizard and Glass*, shortly thereafter, certainly matches the five-book phenomenon of 1986-1987 that Stephanie Leonard referred to in her *Castle Rock* editorial nearly a decade before—to say nothing of the solid works King has published in the intervening years. But *The Tommyknockers* did signal the completion of themes and images he had worked with for over fifteen years. Begun in 1982 and not finished until five years later, *The Tommyknockers* records King's struggles with those themes. And it is a valid conclusion to King's first *annus mirabilis*—a year that saw the publication of *IT*, the revised trade edition of *The Eyes of the Dragon*, *The Drawing of the Three*, and *Misery*. It takes a well-earned place on the shelf, alongside the rest of King's novels, effectively bracketing a part of his life that began with *Rage* and *Carrie* and grew and matured through *The Tommyknockers*.

III.

A BESTSELLING BESTSELLER[1]

At the end of Stephen King's first ten years as a regular on the national bestsellers lists in 1986, he had already set a number of sales records for his novels, including several weeks with an astonishing *five* titles occurring simultaneously on the hardcover, mass-market paperback, and trade paperback lists; a slightly larger number of weeks with four titles; and occurrences of two and three titles so frequent as to barely elicit comment. His collectibles were commanding extraordinary prices; his new books were literally lining bookstore walls on the first days of release; and in some senses he was undeniably among the hottest literary phenomena of the mid-1980s.

By 1996, another decade later, there has been some lessening of King's impact as cultural phenomenon, not so much because his books are less popular or noticeably less frequent residents of the lists, but rather because it has become almost normal for his titles to capture and hold first place on national lists for weeks at a time, then to remain on the lists for even longer stretches. He is still setting records, and one estimate suggests that there are at least 100,000,000 copies of his books in print worldwide.[2] And, with the widespread responses to his serialized novel, *The Green Mile*, it is entirely possible that late 1996 might see King with six simultaneous bestsellers.

Two decades after his first appearance as a national bestseller, Stephen King is still a publishing phenomenon.

Yet to consider Stephen King as a cultural "phenomenon" is inherently more difficult than to discuss his novels, stories, or films. After all, the latter exist as specific, concrete texts or visual images, readily available to critic, reader, or viewer alike; to that extent, there are objective criteria for assessing King's weaknesses and strengths as a writer, his undoubted successes and his putative failures, however personal the criticism itself might become (and with King's novels and stories, criticism occasionally takes on an uncomfortably personal tone). But the idea of a "phenomenon" is subjective and amorphous, lacking that sense of factual solidity so comforting when one works with texts. In addition, much of the material necessary to establish how and why King could be classified as a "phenomenon" is difficult to locate, often requiring hours of research.

Perhaps for that reason it would be wise to base an examination of King as cultural phenomenon on references to specific data and thus establish King as a writer whose works engender literally phenomenal responses in readers. And the most direct way to do that is by looking at some of the statistics available.

King's stories are extraordinarily popular and have been so for at least two decades—that much is obvious to anyone familiar with contemporary publishing. By 1985, for example, he ranked second in the list of authors with the most bestselling titles between 1965 and 1985. For those two decades, Victoria Holt held first place with ten titles, her first, *The Legend of the Seventh Virgin*, appearing on the lists in 1965 and her last, *The Pride of the Peacock*, eleven years later. Stephen King's nine titles (*The Shining* through *The Talisman*) were published in the space of only nine years; and the authors of *American Best Sellers* note that two more titles, *Skeleton Crew* and *IT*, had already reached the lists by the time their manuscript was completed.[3]

But what is perhaps less obvious about Stephen King than the mere numbers is the remarkable extent and durability of his popularity. One of the best ways to assess a writer's immediate impact on the reading public is to review national bestsellers lists based on weekly sales figures accumulated from leading bookstores and other outlets—theoretically, at least, a good proportion of the reading public paying good money for a hardcover novel, or perhaps less for a mass-market or trade paperback, will do so because reading the book in question meets some need, although admittedly a fair number of past bestsellers have receded into literary limbo. Even so, when the number of books reaches the almost unimaginable levels associated with Stephen King, the suggestion is that he is tapping into a powerful undercurrent of need.

Stephen King's name first appeared on a national bestsellers list in August, 1976; at the end of July, 1986, he completed a full decade as a bestseller; at the end of July 1996, he will have completed his second full decade. After analyzing the frequency of appearances for his books during that twenty-year span, one begins to understand just how remarkable King's career has been as he shattered record after record, reaching a first peak in an almost incredible series of entries in late 1985 and early 1986; another peak in early 1988; and a third in April 1996—in each instance having several sequential weeks of four or five simultaneous titles on the lists.

Although there are many bestsellers lists, several of them highly influential and prestigious, three are particularly valuable. *The New York Times Book Review* appears on Sunday and in some ways represents the literary "establishment"; its bestsellers lists are based on nation-wide figures and are often reproduced by smaller papers and bookstores. *The Los Angeles Times Book Review* identifies west-coast regional bestsellers each Sunday, concentrating on the top-selling titles in

45

Southern California; this information frequently coincides with the *New York Times* list but occasionally shows some interesting anomalies. The third listing appears in *Publishers Weekly*, a leading trade journal for booksellers, and is based on reported sales figures compiled from "large-city bookstores, bookstore chains, and local bestseller lists across the U.S." These three represent a fascinating cross-section of interests as well as a wide statistical base for computation.

Each title in this discussion appeared on at least one of these lists for each week in question. Often, of course, a title will appear on all three; but especially during the few weeks at the beginning and end of a title's run on the lists, there is some variation.

Consulting these lists from August 1976 through October 1986, one finds some stunning statistical data relevant to King's appearances.

For one thing, he appears far more frequently than one might expect, even given his immense popularity. During the 520 weeks from August 1976 through July 1986, King's name appears at least *545* times—for an unprecedented average of 1.05 titles *per week* for a full ten years. A decade later, after 1030 weeks since the paperback edition of *'Salem's Lot* first hit the lists, he has had a total of 1,097 entries for a twenty-year average of1.065 titles *per week.*

Of course, his actual appearances are less regular than that; many weeks show no King titles at all, while at other times he appears with multiple titles. For 240 weeks—or almost one-fourth of the total—King was represented by *at least* two titles. But that is only the beginning of the story.

In August of 1981, King made publishing history by becoming the first American writer with *three* titles on the lists simultaneously: the hardcover *Firestarter*, the paperback *The Dead Zone* (which hit number one its first week), and the movie tie-in paperback of *The Shining*. All three appeared for six consecutive weeks, from August 17 to September 28. Since then, King has had *three* titles simultaneously at least thirty-seven times, for a total of forty-three weeks

During the week of October 20, 1985, King broke his own record by having *four* entries: the hardcover *Skeleton Crew*; the mass-market paperback editions of *Thinner* and *The Talisman*; and the trade paperback of *The Bachman Books* (the bestselling trade paperback fiction for the week). Between October 20, 1985 and January 19, 1986, King again had four simultaneous titles, this time for a total of nine weeks. Beginning in mid-May of 1996, he again had four titles—all three of *The Green Mile* installments then published, plus the paperback edition of *Rose Madder*. In total he has had more than thirteen weeks with four simultaneous titles.

Even more remarkably, for three weeks (November 17-31, 1985 and January 12-18, 1986), King shattered all records by having *five* simultaneous entries: the hardcover *Skeleton Crew*; the hardcover

The Bachman Books; mass-market paperback editions of *The Talisman* and *Thinner*; and the trade paperback edition of *The Bachman Books*. Then again in the beginning of January, 1991, he repeated this achievement with the hardcover *Four Past Midnight*, the hardcover *The Stand: The Complete & Uncut Edition*, and the paperback editions of *Misery*, *IT* (the movie tie-in issue), and *The Dark Half*. To date (June 1996), he has had an enviable six weeks with five simultaneous titles. And, given the tenacity with which *The Green Mile* installments are hovering in the first half-dozen slots, it seems likely that July or August, 1996 should add several weeks to that total.

Surely King has made his point—the point that he set out to demonstrate in 1985-1986: multiple publications in a single year, even multiple *hardcover* publications, do not seem to cut into his popularity or sales. In King's case, it means more appearances on every best-sellers list possible.

In addition, King has an impressive record of books reaching number one on the lists. Beginning with *The Dead Zone*, hardcover editions of his works have held that position for well over 113 weeks, over 10% of the weeks for twenty years; paperback editions for over ninety-four weeks; and for twenty weeks, his books ranked number one in both categories simultaneously. The hardcover editions of *Misery*, *The Tommyknockers*, *Four Past Midnight*, *Gerald's Game*, and *Insomnia* reached number one on its first appearance. Several paperbacks also reached number one their first week: *The Dead Zone*, *Firestarter*, *Pet Sematary*, *Skeleton Crew*, *The Dark Tower: The Gunslinger*, *The Dark Tower II: The Drawing of the Three*, *Misery*, *The Green Mile 1: The Two Dead Girls*, *The Green Mile 2: The Mouse on the Mile*, and *The Green Mile 3: Coffey's Hands*. In total, King has had number-one bestsellers for an unprecedented total of well over 200 weeks.

Two titles mentioned above also indicate another perspective on King as publishing phenomenon. Many writers reach the bestsellers lists with novels; King has done so with novels, nonfiction (*Danse Macabre*), and, more unusually, collections of short fiction. *Night Shift* appeared on the paperback lists for thirteen weeks; *Different Seasons* was included on hardcover and paperback lists for forty-four weeks; *Skeleton Crew* was garnered an equal total of forty-four, including a total of fifteen weeks at the top. *The Bachman Books*, a collection of four short novels published several years before, stayed on the 1985-1986 charts for nineteen weeks. *Four Past Midnight* hit first place in its first week in hardcover and remained on the lists for forty-one weeks. And King's most recent collection, *Nightmares & Dreamscapes*, acquitted itself more than creditably with sixteen weeks as a hardcover bestseller and seven in paperback. Normally, fiction collections simply do not sell well enough to reach bestsellers lists; in King's case, *Skeleton Crew*, *The Bachman Books*, and *Four Past Midnight* not only made the lists but reached number one.

The following chart reproduces the number of weeks each King title has appeared on bestseller lists. The first figure represents hardcover editions; the second, mass-market or trade paperbacks; the third, total weeks on the charts; and fourth, total weeks at number one in hardcover (hc) and paperback (p):

	HC	PB	Tot.	#1 hc	#1 pb	Tot.
Carrie	-	14	14	1	-	-
'Salem's Lot	-	15	15	-	2	2
The Shining	6	30	36	-	-	-
The Stand	6	16	22	-	2	2
Night Shift	-	13	13	-	-	-
The Dead Zone	37	13	50	2	5	7
Firestarter	40	13	53	4	5	9
Danse Macabre	10	-	10	-	-	-
Cujo	35	10	45	5	2	7
Different Seasons	34	10	44	-	-	-
Christine	31	15	46	-	8	8
Pet Sematary	30	20	50	9	3	12
The Talisman	27	14	41	11	4	15
Thinner	24	17	41	1	5	6
Cycle of the Werewolf	-	7	7	-	-	-
Skeleton Crew	33	10	43	9	6	15
The Bachman Books	3	19	21	-	7	7
IT	35	28	63	11	7	18
Eyes of the Dragon	23	11	34	-	4	4
Misery	33	13	46	7	1	8
The Tommyknockers	23	13	36	8	3	11
The Dark Tower:						
The Gunslinger	-	34	34	-	5	5
The Dark Tower II: The						
Drawing of the Three	-	31	31	-	3	3
The Dark Half	16	18	34	10	4	14
The Stand: Complete &						
Uncut Edition	27	12	39	4	-	4
Four Past Midnight	22	19	41	5	2	7
Needful Things	20	14	34	-	-	-
The Dark Tower III:						
The Waste Lands	-	14	14	-	1	-
Gerald's Game	20	11	33	9	0	9
Dolores Claiborne	13	8	21	5	1	6
Nightmares &						
Dreamscapes	16	7	23	-	-	-

Insomnia	14	9	23	3	-	-
Rose Madder	11	7	18	2	-	2
The Green Mile 1: The *Two Dead Girls*	-	13	13	-	5	5
The Green Mile 2: The *Mouse on the Mile*	-	9	9	-	5	5
The Green Mile 3: *Coffey's Hands*	-	5	5	-	4	4

[NOTE: Data are current through the week ending June 30, 1996.]

The sheer numbers of books printed are impressive as well. *Publishers Weekly* occasionally updates the total number of copies for titles on the weekly lists. In King's case, the numbers spiral:

▶ His first title to reach the lists, the paperback *'Salem's Lot*, had seen five printings totaling 1,370,000 copies when it first appeared in ninth place on the *PW* list on August 23, 1976. Booksellers reported the novel as selling 50,000 copies a day. A week later, the sixth printing brought the number of copies to 1,400,000. It last appeared on the lists during the week of November 28, 1976; it had reached its twentieth printing, with 2,200,000 copies.

▶ The movie tie-in paperback of *Carrie* hit the lists on December 5, 1976 and remained there for fourteen weeks. By March, 1977, it had reached twenty-four printings and 2,900,000 copies.

▶ The paperback *The Shining* first reached the lists in mid-January, 1978. By February 6, it had reached six printings and 2,025,000 copies. On March 20, *PW* reported ten printings and 2,265,000 copies.

▶ In late August, 1979, the hardcover edition of *The Dead Zone* placed eleventh on the lists; it already had 110,000 copies in print *before* the official publication date, August 30, 1979. Within two months, it reached its eighth printing and a total of 200,000 copies.

▶ In June, 1980, *The Shining* was released as a paperback movie tie-in. By June 20, 1980, it had reached its eighteenth printing, for a total of 4,100,000 copies. Seven weeks later, a twenty-first printing resulted in 4,400,000 copies.

▶   By the time the hardcover *Firestarter* had been on the lists for seventeen weeks (December 12, 1980), it had been reprinted five times for a total of 275,000 copies. A sixth printing in January, 1981, brought the total to 285,000. The paperback edition had 2,750,000 copies in print when it first reached the lists in August, 1981.

▶   The hardcover *Cujo* was reprinted three times *before* its official publication date on September 8, 1981, with 300,000 copies already already in print. By December, the number had increased to over 360,000 copies. On August 6, 1982, the paperback edition reached fourth place on the lists, after three printings totaling 2,470,000 copies. A fourth printing three weeks later raised that figure to 2,525,000 copies. The movie tie-in edition in September, 1983, raised the total to 3,160,000.

▶   In its first appearance on the lists in mid-April, 1982, the hardcover *Christine* boasted 325,000 copies in print. The paperback appeared as number eleven on the lists on November 25, 1983, already totaling over 2,900,000 copies in print.

▶   The hardcover *Pet Sematary* had a first printing of 350,000 copies. On its third week on the lists, a fourth printing raised the total to 575,000. The paperback appeared in third position on November 2, 1984 with 2,667,000 copies already in print. By May, 1989, the book had 4,400,000 copies in print and reappeared on the paperback lists for five more weeks.

▶   *The Talisman* set publication records with a 600,000 first printing. It appeared on the *PW* list on November 2, 1984, hitting number one the first week. By November 8, an additional printing brought the total to 705,000—and this for a hardcover novel then retailing at $18.95.

▶   By September, 1985, there were 2,500,000 paperback copies of *Thinner* in print. Eight weeks later, the total was 3,050,000.

▶   *The Bachman Books* appeared in fourth place on the trade paperback lists in October, 1985, with a total of 600,000 copies.

▶   *IT* broke the record set by *The Talisman* for a first printing—with 860,000 copies, not including the German-language limited edition of 250 published in Munich as *ES* almost five months before the Viking trade edition. By the time the mass-market paperback appeared on the lists in August, 1987, there were over 2,650,000 copies in print.

▸ *The Bachman Books* appeared on the paperback bestsellers lists in November, 1986, with 2,250,000 copies in print.

▸ *The Eyes of the Dragon* appeared on the lists in February, 1987, with a 1,000,000 copy first printing, exceeding the record set by *IT*.

▸ *Misery* appeared in June, 1987, with a 900,000 copy first printing; by the time the mass market paperback appeared a year later, there were over 3,000,000 copies in print.

▸ *The Tommyknockers* appeared on the hardcover lists in December, 1987, with 1,200,000 copies; less than a year later, the mass-market paperback appeared on the lists, with a total of 3,100,000 copies in print.

▸ After years as one of the least accessible (hence most collectible) King titles, *The Dark Tower: The Gunslinger* appeared as a trade paperback in October, 1988, with a 1,200,000 print run, and immediately ranked first in the week's bestseller lists. When *The Dark Tower II: The Drawing of the Three* appeared as a trade paperback, with a print run of 925,000 copies, it not only held first place on the lists for three weeks, but it also stimulated a renewed interest in *The Dark Tower: The Gunslinger*, which reappeared and remained on the lists for six additional weeks in mid-1989.

▸ *The Dark Half* again saw an increase in print-run, appearing in hardcover in November 1989 with 1,500,000 copies and appearing second on the lists; by the second week, it ranked as number one.

▸ When *The Dark Tower: The Drawing of the Three* appeared as a mass-market paperback in January, 1990, records showed over 2,500,000 copies in print.

▸ *The Stand: The Complete and Uncut Edition* appeared on the lists in May, 1990, with 500,000 copies in print; the book became the seventh ranked bestselling fiction title for 1990, with 653,828 copies in print. The original edition of *The Stand* had not even reached the top twenty-five in sales.

▶ Richard Hendricks has estimated that in 1992 *alone*, sales for six King titles—*Dolores Claiborne, Gerald's Game, The Dark Tower III: The Waste Lands, Four Past Midnight, Needful Things,* and *The Stand: The Complete & Uncut Edition* (which Hendricks refers to as a "mass market doorstop")—totalled in excess of 11, 265,000 copies. He further estimates returns of between $80 and $110 million on those books. "Of course," he adds, "S.K. doesn't *make* all this money, but it certainly puts the gross national product of many small countries to shame."[4]

While few of King's more recent novels have matched the enduring popularity of *The Dead Zone* or *The Stand,* they nevertheless continue to recur on bestsellers lists.

More directly, perhaps, a cursory examination of local bookshelves reveals that as of June 1996, reprints of paperback editions had reached equally impressive numbers:

Novel	Paperback and Hardcover Printings to June 1996
Carrie	70
'Salem's Lot	57
The Shining	56
(hardcover edition):	17
*The Stand**	13
(hardcover edition):	11
Night Shift	59
The Dead Zone	45
(hardcover edition):	16
Firestarter	31
Cujo	33
Danse Macabre	35
Different Seasons	40
(hardcover edition):	13
The Dark Tower: The Gunslinger	24
Christine	29
(hardcover edition):	7
Cycle of the Werewolf	8
Pet Sematary	43
The Eyes of the Dragon	28
The Talisman	22
Thinner	25
Skeleton Crew	30
The Bachman Books	16
IT	35
Misery	36

*The information is for *The Stand: The Complete & Uncut Edition*, published in 1990; the original edition had reach 25 printings by mid-1986.

A further indication of King's standing in the industry appears in the total sales figures compiled yearly by *Publishers Weekly*. In 1985 King's name figured prominently. King and Danielle Steel both appeared *twice* on the hardcover list. *Skeleton Crew*, a collection of short stories no less, ranked fifth, with total sales of 600,000 copies. *Thinner* placed eleventh, with sales of 300,000 copies. However, 1985 was not the first year that two King titles appeared simultaneously. In 1983, both *Pet Sematary* (with 657,741 copies sold) and *Christine* ranked in the top fifteen in sales. Only three other writers have had two titles on year-end hardcover lists: Frederick Forsyth in 1972, John O'Hara in 1960, and James Hilton in 1935.[5] *The Bachman Books* did not make the cut-off at fifteen, but did appear in a supplemental listing of fiction selling in excess of 100,000 copies in 1985.

In paperback sales, King's presence was again clearly felt. The top-selling novel for 1985 was V. C. Andrews's *Seeds of Yesterday*, with 3,550,000 copies. Third place went to Danielle Steel's *Full Circle*, at 3,234,934 copies. King, however, took both second and fourth place: *Pet Sematary* sold 3,275,000 copies, and *Thinner* 3,050,000 copies. *The Talisman* ranked eighth for the year, at 2,700,000 copies.

Even in trade paperbacks, King made a strong showing. Two of the top three bestsellers for 1985 were King titles: *The Bachman Books* (800,000 copies) and *Cycle of the Werewolf* (765,000 copies).

Total sales for just these nine volumes exceeded 11,500,000 copies—and all of this in just one year. In the decade since 1986, sales of King's books has continued almost as strongly, including several more best-of-the-year sales records in both hardcover and paperback. King's record as a bestseller is impressive—indeed, it is record-breaking and unprecedented in almost every instance.

The following pages list each appearance of a King title on national bestsellers lists from *The New York Times Book Review*, *The Los Angeles Times Book Review*, and *Publishers Weekly*. It is one thing to read bare statistical data—percentages of weeks appearing, number of weeks at number one, etc. It is something else again to see that information represented graphically and realize how often King's works have been represented.

Titles printed in boldface type and preceded by an asterisk placed number one for the week in at least one list; dates printed in boldface type and followed by an asterisk indicate weeks during which King had at least *three* titles on the lists simultaneously—one asterisk for three simultaneous titles, two asterisks for four, and three asterisks for five. For ease in reading the chart, all dates have been regularized to begin on Sunday—the day *The New York Times Book Review* and *The Los Angeles Times Book Review* appear (*Publishers Weekly* lists appear on Fridays and are listed under the preceding Sunday).

TABLE I

STEPHEN KING BESTSELLERS

Week of:	Hardcover	Paperback
1976		
22 Aug 76		*'Salem's Lot*
29 Aug 76		*'Salem's Lot*
5 Sep 76		*'Salem's Lot*
12 Sep 76		*'Salem's Lot*
19 Sep 76		*'Salem's Lot*
26 Sep 76		****'Salem's Lot***
3 Oct 76		****'Salem's Lot***
10 Oct 76		*'Salem's Lot*
17 Oct 76		*'Salem's Lot*
24 Oct 76		*'Salem's Lot*
31 Oct 76		*'Salem's Lot*
7 Nov 76		*'Salem's Lot*
14 Nov 76		*'Salem's Lot*
21 Nov 76		*'Salem's Lot*
28 Nov 76		*'Salem's Lot*
5 Dec 76		*Carrie*
12 Dec 76		*Carrie*
19 Dec 76		*Carrie*
26 Dec 76		*Carrie*
1977		
2 Jan 77		*Carrie*
9 Jan 77		*Carrie*
16 Jan 77		*Carrie*
22 Jan 77		*Carrie*
30 Jan 77		*Carrie*
6 Feb 77		*Carrie*
13 Feb 77		*Carrie*
20 Feb 77		*Carrie*
27 Feb 77	*The Shining*	*Carrie*

6 Mar 77	*The Shining*	*Carrie*
13 Mar 77	*The Shining*	
20 Mar 77	*The Shining*	
27 Mar 77	*The Shining*	
3 Apr 77	*The Shining*	

10 Apr 77-25 Dec 1977: **None**

1978

1 Jan 78-15 Jan 78: **None**

22 Jan 78	*The Shining*
5 Feb 78	*The Shining*
12 Feb 78	*The Shining*
19 Feb 78	*The Shining*
26 Feb 78	*The Shining*
5 Mar 78	*The Shining*
12 Mar 78	*The Shining*
19 Mar 78	*The Shining*
26 Mar 78	*The Shining*
2 Apr 78	*The Shining*
9 Apr 78	*The Shining*
16 Apr 78	*The Shining*
23 Apr 78	*The Shining*
30 Apr 78	*The Shining*
7 May 78	*The Shining*

14 May 78-24 Dec 78: **None**

31 Dec 78   *The Stand*

1979

7 Jan 79	*The Stand*
14 Jan 79: **None**	
21 Jan 79	*The Stand*
28 Jan 79	*The Stand*
4 Feb 79: **None**	
11 Feb 79	*The Stand*
18 Feb 79	*The Stand*
25 Feb 79	*Night Shift*
4 Mar 79	*Night Shift*
11 Mar 79	*Night Shift*
18 Mar 79	*Night Shift*
25 Mar 79	*Night Shift*

1 Apr 79		*Night Shift*
8 Apr 79		*Night Shift*
15 Apr 79		*Night Shift*
22 Apr 79		*Night Shift*
6 May 79		*Night Shift*
13 May 79		*Night Shift*
20 May 79		*Night Shift*

27 May 79-3 Jun 79: **None**

10 Jun 79		*Night Shift*

17 Jun 79-19 Aug 79: **None**

26 Aug 79	*The Dead Zone*

2 Sep 79: **None**

9 Sep 79	*The Dead Zone*
16 Sep 79	*The Dead Zone*
23 Sep 79	*The Dead Zone*
30 Aug 79	*The Dead Zone*
7 Oct 79	*The Dead Zone*
14 Oct 79	***The Dead Zone**
21 Oct 79	***The Dead Zone**
28 Oct 79	*The Dead Zone*
4 Nov 79	*The Dead Zone*
11 Nov 79	*The Dead Zone*
18 Nov 79	*The Dead Zone*
25 Nov 79	*The Dead Zone*
2 Dec 79	*The Dead Zone*
9 Dec 79	*The Dead Zone*
16 Dec 79	*The Dead Zone*
23 Dec 79	*The Dead Zone*
30 Dec 79	*The Dead Zone*

1980

6 Jan 80	*The Dead Zone*	
13 Jan 80	*The Dead Zone*	
20 Jan 80	*The Dead Zone*	*The Stand*
27 Jan 80	*The Dead Zone*	
3 Feb 80	*The Dead Zone*	***The Stand**
10 Feb 80	*The Dead Zone*	***The Stand**
17 Feb 80	*The Dead Zone*	*The Stand*
24 Feb 80	*The Dead Zone*	*The Stand*
2 Mar 80	*The Dead Zone*	*The Stand*
9 Mar 80	*The Dead Zone*	*The Stand*

16 Mar 80	*The Dead Zone*	*The Stand*
23 Mar 80	*The Dead Zone*	*The Stand*
30 Mar 80	*The Dead Zone*	*The Stand*
6 Apr 80	*The Dead Zone*	*The Stand*
13 Apr 80	*The Dead Zone*	*The Stand*
20 Apr 80	*The Dead Zone*	*The Stand*
27 Apr 80	*The Dead Zone*	*The Stand*
4 May 80	*The Dead Zone*	*The Stand*
11 May 80	*The Dead Zone*	*The Stand*

18 May 80-8 Jun 80: **None**

15 Jun 80		*The Shining*
22 Jun 80		*The Shining*
29 Jun 80		*The Shining*
6 Jul 80		*The Shining*
13 Jul 80		*The Shining*
20 Jul 80		*The Shining*
27 Jul 80		*The Shining*
3 Aug 80		*The Shining*
10 Aug 80		*The Shining*
17 Aug 80*	*Firestarter*	**The Dead Zone*
		The Shining
24 Aug 80*	*Firestarter*	**The Dead Zone*
		The Shining
31 Aug 80*	*Firestarter*	**The Dead Zone*
		The Shining
7 Sep 80*	*Firestarter*	**The Dead Zone*
		The Shining
14 Sep 80*	*Firestarter*	**The Dead Zone*
		The Shining
21 Sep 80*	**Firestarter*	*The Dead Zone*
		The Shining
28 Sep 80	**Firestarter*	*The Dead Zone*
5 Oct 80	**Firestarter*	*The Dead Zone*
12 Oct 80	**Firestarter*	*The Dead Zone*
19 Oct 80	*Firestarter*	*The Dead Zone*
26 Oct 80	*Firestarter*	*The Dead Zone*
2 Nov 80	*Firestarter*	*The Dead Zone*
9 Nov 80	*Firestarter*	*The Dead Zone*
16 Nov 80	*Firestarter*	
23 Nov 80	*Firestarter*	
30 Nov 80	*Firestarter*	
7 Dec 80	*Firestarter*	
14 Dec 80	*Firestarter*	
21 Dec 80	*Firestarter*	

28 Dec 80	*Firestarter*

1981

4 Jan 81	*Firestarter*
11 Jan 81	*Firestarter*
18 Jan 81	*Firestarter*
25 Jan 81	*Firestarter*
1 Feb 81	*Firestarter*
8 Feb 81	*Firestarter*
15 Feb 81	*Firestarter*
22 Feb 81	*Firestarter*
1 Mar 81	*Firestarter*
8 Mar 81	*Firestarter*
15 Mar 81	*Firestarter*
22 Mar 81	*Firestarter*
29 Mar 81	*Firestarter*
5 Apr 81	*Firestarter*
12 Apr 81	*Firestarter*
19 Apr 81	*Firestarter*
	Danse Macabre
26 Apr 81	*Firestarter*
	Danse Macabre
3 May 81	*Firestarter*
	Danse Macabre
10 May 81	*Danse Macabre*
17 May 81	*Firestarter*
	Danse Macabre
24 May 81	*Firestarter*
	Danse Macabre
31 May 81	*Danse Macabre*
7 Jun 81	*Danse Macabre*
14 Jun 81	*Danse Macabre*
21 Jun 81	*Danse Macabre*

28 Jun 81-2 Aug 81: **None**

9 Aug 81	*Cujo*	***Firestarter**
16 Aug 81	*Cujo*	***Firestarter**
23 Aug 81	***Cujo**	***Firestarter**
30 Aug 81	***Cujo**	***Firestarter**
6 Sep 81	***Cujo**	***Firestarter**
13 Sep 81	***Cujo**	*Firestarter*
20 Sep 81	***Cujo**	*Firestarter*
27 Sep 81	*Cujo*	*Firestarter*
4 Oct 81	*Cujo*	*Firestarter*

59

11 Oct 81	*Cujo*	*Firestarter*
18 Oct 81	*Cujo*	*Firestarter*
25 Oct 81	*Cujo*	*Firestarter*
1 Nov 81	*Cujo*	*Firestarter*
8 Nov 81	*Cujo*	
15 Nov 81	*Cujo*	
22 Nov 81	*Cujo*	
29 Nov 81	*Cujo*	
6 Dec 81	*Cujo*	
13 Dec 81	*Cujo*	
20 Dec 81	*Cujo*	
27 Dec 81	*Cujo*	

1982

3 Jan 82	*Cujo*
10 Jan 82	*Cujo*
17 Jan 82	*Cujo*
24 Jan 82	*Cujo*
31 Jan 82	*Cujo*
7 Feb 82	*Cujo*
14 Feb 82	*Cujo*
21 Feb 82	*Cujo*
28 Feb 82	*Cujo*
7 Mar 82	*Cujo*
14 Mar 82	*Cujo*
21 Mar 82	*Cujo*
28 Mar 82	*Cujo*
4 Apr 82	*Cujo*

11 Apr 82-1 Aug 82: **None**

8 Aug 82	*Different Seasons*	*Cujo*
15 Aug 82	*Different Seasons*	***Cujo**
22 Aug 82	*Different Seasons*	***Cujo**
29 Aug 82	*Different Seasons*	*Cujo*
5 Sep 82	*Different Seasons*	*Cujo*
12 Sep 82	*Different Seasons*	*Cujo*
19 Sep 82	*Different Seasons*	*Cujo*
26 Sep 82	*Different Seasons*	*Cujo*
3 Oct 82	*Different Seasons*	*Cujo*
10 Oct 82	*Different Seasons*	
17 Oct 82	*Different Seasons*	
24 Oct 82	*Different Seasons*	
31 Oct 82	*Different Seasons*	
7 Nov 82	*Different Seasons*	

14 Nov 82	*Different Seasons*	
21 Nov 82	*Different Seasons*	
28 Nov 82	*Different Seasons*	
5 Dec 82	*Different Seasons*	
12 Dec 82	*Different Seasons*	
19 Dec 82	*Different Seasons*	
26 Dec 82	*Different Seasons*	

1983

2 Jan 83	*Different Seasons*	
9 Jan 83	*Different Seasons*	
16 Jan 83	*Different Seasons*	
23 Jan 83	*Different Seasons*	
30 Jan 83	*Different Seasons*	
6 Feb 83	*Different Seasons*	
13 Feb 83	*Different Seasons*	
20 Feb 83	*Different Seasons*	
27 Feb 83	*Different Seasons*	
6 Mar 83	*Different Seasons*	
13 Mar 83	*Different Seasons*	
20 Mar 83	*Different Seasons*	
27 Mar 83	*Different Seasons*	
3 Apr 83: **None**		
10 Apr 83	*Christine*	
17 Apr 83	*Christine*	
25 Apr 83	*Christine*	
1 May 83	*Christine*	
8 May 83	*Christine*	
15 May 83	*Christine*	
22 May 83	*Christine*	
29 May 83	*Christine*	
5 Jun 83	*Christine*	
12 Jun 83	*Christine*	
19 Jun 83	*Christine*	
26 Jun 83	*Christine*	
3 Jul 83	*Christine*	
10 Jul 83	*Christine*	
17 Jul 83	*Christine*	
24 Jul 83	*Christine*	
31 Jul 83	*Christine*	
7 Aug 83	*Christine*	*Different Seasons*
14 Aug 83	*Christine*	*Different Seasons*
21 Aug 83	*Christine*	*Different Seasons*
28 Aug 83*	*Christine*	*Different Seasons*
		Cujo

4 Sep 83	*Christine*	*Different Seasons*
11 Sep 83	*Christine*	*Different Seasons*
18 Sep 83	*Christine*	*Different Seasons*
25 Sep 83	*Christine*	*Different Seasons*
2 Oct 83	*Christine*	*Different Seasons*
9 Oct 83	*Christine*	*Different Seasons*
16 Oct 83	*Christine*	
23 Oct 83	*Christine*	
30 Oct 83	*Christine*	
6 Nov 83	*Christine*	
13 Nov 83	*Pet Sematary*	
	Christine	
20 Nov 83	***Pet Sematary***	*Christine*
27 Nov B3	***Pet Sematary***	***Christine***
4 Dec 83	***Pet Sematary***	***Christine***
11 Dec 83	***Pet Sematary***	***Christine***
18 Dec 83	***Pet Sematary***	***Christine***
25 Dec 83	***Pet Sematary***	***Christine***

1984

1 Jan 84	*Pet Sematary*	***Christine***
8 Jan 84	*Pet Sematary*	***Christine***
15 Jan 84	***Pet Sematary***	***Christine***
22 Jan 84	***Pet Sematary***	*Christine*
29 Jan 84	***Pet Sematary***	*Christine*
5 Feb 84	***Pet Sematary***	*Christine*
12 Feb 84	***Pet Sematary***	*Christine*
19 Feb 84	***Pet Sematary***	*Christine*
26 Feb 84	***Pet Sematary***	
4 Mar 84	***Pet Sematary***	
11 Mar 84	***Pet Sematary***	
18 Mar 84	*Pet Sematary*	
25 Mar 84	*Pet Sematary*	
1 Apr 84	*Pet Sematary*	
8 Apr 84	*Pet Sematary*	
15 Apr 84	*Pet Sematary*	
22 Apr 84	*Pet Sematary*	
29 Apr 84	*Pet Sematary*	
6 May 84	*Pet Sematary*	
13 May 84	*Pet Sematary*	
20 May 84	*Pet Sematary*	
27 May 84	*Pet Sematary*	
3 Jun 84	*Pet Sematary*	

10 Jun 84-14 Oct 84: **None**

21 Oct 84	*The Talisman*	
28 Oct 84	*The Talisman*	***Pet Sematary***
4 Nov 84	***The Talisman***	***Pet Sematary***
11 Nov 84	***The Talisman***	***Pet Sematary***
18 Nov 84	***The Talisman***	*Pet Sematary*
25 Nov 84	***The Talisman***	*Pet Sematary*
2 Dec 84	***The Talisman***	*Pet Sematary*
9 Dec 84	***The Talisman***	*Pet Sematary*
16 Dec 84	***The Talisman***	*Pet Sematary*
23 Dec 84	, ***The Talisman***	*Pet Sematary*
30 Dec 84	***The Talisman***	*Pet Sematary*

1985

6 Jan 85	***The Talisman***	*Pet Sematary*
13 Jan 85	***The Talisman***	*Pet Sematary*
20 Jan 85	*The Talisman*	*Pet Sematary*
27 Jan 85	*The Talisman*	*Pet Sematary*
3 Feb 85	*The Talisman*	*Pet Sematary*
10 Feb 85	*The Talisman*	
17 Feb 85	*The Talisman*	
24 Feb 85	*The Talisman*	
3 Mar 85	*The Talisman* *Thinner*	
10 Mar 85	*The Talisman* *Thinner*	
17 Mar 85	*Thinner* *The Talisman*	
24 Mar 85	*Thinner* *The Talisman*	
31 Mar 85	*Thinner* *The Talisman*	
7 Apr 85	*Thinner* *The Talisman*	
14 Apr 85	*Thinner* *The Talisman*	
21 Apr 85	*Thinner* *The Talisman*	
28 Apr 85	*Thinner*	
5 May 85	***Thinner***	*Cycle of the Werewolf*
12 May 85	*Thinner*	*Cycle of the Werewolf*
19 May 85	*Thinner*	*Cycle of the Werewolf*
26 May 85*	*Thinner* *The Talisman*	*Cycle of the Werewolf*
2 Jun 85	*Thinner*	*Cycle of the Werewolf*
9 Jun 85	*Thinner*	*Cycle of the Werewolf*

16 Jun 85*	*Thinner*	*Cycle of the Werewolf*
	Skeleton Crew	
23 Jun 85	*Skeleton Crew*	
	Thinner	
30 Jun 85	***Skeleton Crew***	
	Thinner	
7 Jul 85	***Skeleton Crew***	
	Thinner	
14 Jul 85	***Skeleton Crew***	
	Thinner	
21 Jul 85	***Skeleton Crew***	
	Thinner	
28 Jul 85	***Skeleton Crew***	
	Thinner	
4 Aug 85	***Skeleton Crew***	
	Thinner	
11 Aug 85	***Skeleton Crew***	
	Thinner	
18 Aug 85	***Skeleton Crew***	
25 Aug 85	***Skeleton Crew***	
1 Sep 85	*Skeleton Crew*	*Thinner*
8 Sep 85	*Skeleton Crew*	***Thinner***
15 Sep 85	*Skeleton Crew*	***Thinner***
22 Sep 85	*Skeleton Crew*	***Thinner***
29 Sep 85	*Skeleton Crew*	***Thinner***
6 Oct 85	*Skeleton Crew*	***Thinner***
13 Oct 85*	*Skeleton Crew*	*Thinner*
		The Bachman Books
20 Oct 85*	*Skeleton Crew*	***The Bachman Books***
		Thinner
27 Oct 85**	*Skeleton Crew*	***The Bachman Books***
		Thinner
		The Talisman
3 Nov 85**	*Skeleton Crew*	***The Bachman Books***
		Thinner
		The Talisman
10 Nov 85**	*Skeleton Crew*	***The Talisman***
		The Bachman Books
		Thinner
17 Nov 85**	*Skeleton Crew*	*The Bachman Books*
	The Bachman Books	***The Talisman***
		Thinner
24 Nov 85**	*Skeleton Crew*	***The Talisman***
	The Bachman Books	***The Bachman Books***
		Thinner
1 Dec 85**	*Skeleton Crew*	***The Bachman Books***

		The Talisman
		Thinner
8 Dec 85**	Skeleton Crew	**The Talisman*
		*The Bachman Books
		Thinner
15 Dec 85**	Skeleton Crew	**The Bachman Books*
		The Talisman
		Thinner
22 Dec 85*	Skeleton Crew	The Talisman
		The Bachman Books
29 Dec 85*	Skeleton Crew	The Talisman
		The Bachman Books

1986

5 Jan 86*	Skeleton Crew	The Talisman
		The Bachman Books
12 Jan 86**	Skeleton Crew	The Talisman
	The Bachman Books	The Bachman Books
		Thinner
19 Jan 86*	Skeleton Crew	The Talisman
		The Bachman Books
26 Jan 86*	Skeleton Crew	The Talisman
		The Bachman Books

2 Feb 86-18 May 86: **None**

25 May 86	**Skeleton Crew*
1 Jun 86	Skeleton Crew
8 Jun 86	**Skeleton Crew*
15 Jun 86	**Skeleton Crew*
22 Jun 86	**Skeleton Crew*
29 Jun 86	**Skeleton Crew*
6 Jul 86	**Skeleton Crew*
13 Jul 86	Skeleton Crew
20 Jul 86	Skeleton Crew
27 Jul 86	Skeleton Crew
3 Aug 86	Skeleton Crew

10 Aug 86-24 Aug 86: **None**

31 Aug 86	IT
7 Sep 86	IT
14 Sep 86	**IT*
21 Sep 86	**IT*
28 Sep 86	**IT*

5 Oct 86	*IT	
12 Oct 86	*IT	
19 Oct 86	*IT	
26 Oct 86	*IT	
2 Nov 86	*IT	The Bachman Books
9 Nov 86	IT	The Bachman Books
16 Nov 86	IT	The Bachman Books
23 Nov 86	IT	The Bachman Books
30 Nov 86	IT	The Bachman Books
7 Dec 86	IT	
14 Dec 86	IT	
21 Dec 86	IT	
28 Dec 86	*IT	

1987

6 Jan 87	*IT
13 Jan 87	*IT
20 Jan 87	IT
27 Jan 87	IT
2 Feb 87	The Eyes of the Dragon IT
8 Feb 87	The Eyes of the Dragon IT
15 Feb 87	The Eyes of the Dragon IT
22 Feb 87	The Eyes of the Dragon IT
1 Mar 87	The Eyes of the Dragon IT
8 Mar 87	The Eyes of the Dragon IT
15 Mar 87	The Eyes of the Dragon IT
22 Mar 87	The Eyes of the Dragon IT
29 Mar 87	The Eyes of the Dragon IT
5 Apr 87	The Eyes of the Dragon IT
12 Apr 87	The Eyes of the Dragon IT
19 Apr 87	The Eyes of the Dragon IT
26 Apr 87	The Eyes of the Dragon IT

3 May 87	*The Eyes of the Dragon*	
10 May 87	*The Eyes of the Dragon*	
17 May 87	*The Eyes of the Dragon*	
24 May 87	*The Eyes of the Dragon*	
31 May 87	*The Eyes of the Dragon*	
7 Jun 87	***Misery***	
	The Eyes of the Dragon	
14 Jun 87	***Misery***	
	The Eyes of the Dragon	
21 Jun 87	***Misery***	
	The Eyes of the Dragon	
28 Jun 87	***Misery***	
	The Eyes of the Dragon	
5 Jul 87	***Misery***	
	The Eyes of the Dragon	
12 Jul 87	***Misery***	
19 Jul 87	***Misery***	
26 Jul 87	*Misery*	
2 Aug 87	*Misery*	
9 Aug 87	*Misery*	
16 Aug 87	*Misery*	
23 Aug 87	*Misery*	*IT*
30 Aug 87	*Misery*	***IT***
6 Sep 87	*Misery*	***IT***
13 Sep 87	*Misery*	***IT***
20 Sep 87	*Misery*	***IT***
27 Sep 87	*Misery*	***IT***
4 Oct 87	*Misery*	***IT***
11 Oct 87	*Misery*	***IT***
18 Oct 87	*Misery*	*IT*
25 Oct 87	*Misery*	*IT*
1 Nov 87	*Misery*	*IT*
8 Nov 87	*Misery*	*IT*
15 Nov 87	*Misery*	*IT*
22 Nov 87	*Misery*	*IT*
29 Nov 87	***The Tommyknockers***	*IT*
	Misery	
6 Dec 87	***The Tommyknockers***	
	Misery	
13 Dec 87	***The Tommyknockers***	
	Misery	
20 Dec 87	***The Tommyknockers***	
	Misery	
27 Dec 87	***The Tommyknockers***	
	Misery	

1988

3 Jan 88**	*The Tommyknockers*	*The Eyes of the Dragon*
	Misery	*IT*
10 Jan 88**	*The Tommyknockers*	*The Eyes of the Dragon*
	Misery	*IT*
17 Jan 88**	*The Tommyknockers*	*The Eyes of the Dragon*
	Misery	*IT*
24 Jan 88*	*The Tommyknockers*	*The Eyes of the Dragon*
		IT
21 Jan 88*	*The Tommyknockers*	*The Eyes of the Dragon*
		IT
7 Feb 88*	*The Tommyknockers*	*The Eyes of the Dragon*
		IT
14 Feb 88	*The Tommyknockers*	*The Eyes of the Dragon*
21 Feb 88	*The Tommyknockers*	*The Eyes of the Dragon*
28 Feb 88	*The Tommyknockers*	*The Eyes of the Dragon*
6 Mar 88	*The Tommyknockers*	*The Eyes of the Dragon*
13 Mar 88	*The Tommyknockers*	*The Eyes of the Dragon*
20 Mar 88	*The Tommyknockers*	
27 Mar 88	*The Tommyknockers*	
3 Apr 88	*The Tommyknockers*	
10 Apr 88	*The Tommyknockers*	
17 Apr 88	*The Tommyknockers*	
24 Apr 88	*The Tommyknockers*	
1 May 88	*The Tommyknockers*	

8 May 88-22 May 88: **None**

29 May 88	*Misery*
5 June 88	*Misery*
12 June 88	*Misery*
19 June 88	*Misery*
26 June 88	*Misery*
3 July 88	*Misery*
10 July 88	*Misery*
17 July 88	*Misery*
24 July 88	*Misery*
31 July 88	*Misery*
7 Aug 88	*Misery*
14 Aug 88	*Misery*
21 Aug 88	*Misery*

28 Aug 88-2 Oct 88: **None**

9 Oct 88	*The Dark Tower: The Gunslinger*

16 Oct 88	*The Dark Tower*
23 Oct 88	*The Dark Tower*
30 Oct 88	*The Dark Tower*
6 Nov 88	*The Dark Tower*
13 Nov 88	The Tommyknockers
	The Dark Tower
20 Nov 88	The Tommyknockers
	The Dark Tower
27 Nov 88	*The Tommyknockers*
	The Dark Tower
4 Dec 88	*The Tommyknockers*
	The Dark Tower
11 Dec 88	The Tommyknockers
	The Dark Tower
18 Dec 88	The Tommyknockers
	The Dark Tower
25 Dec 88	The Tommyknockers
	The Dark Tower

1989

1 Jan 89	The Tommyknockers
	The Dark Tower
8 Jan 89	*Tommyknockers*
	The Dark Tower
15 Jan 89	The Tommyknockers
	The Dark Tower
22 Jan 89	The Tommyknockers
29 Jan 89	The Tommyknockers
5 Feb 89	The Tommyknockers

12 Feb 89-16 Apr 89: **None**

23 Apr 89	*The Dark Tower II: The Drawing of the Three*
	The Dark Tower
30 Apr 89	*The Dark Tower II*
	The Dark Tower
7 May 89	*The Dark Tower II*
	The Dark Tower
14 May 89*	Pet Sematary
	The Dark Tower II
	The Dark Tower
21 May 89*	Pet Sematary
	The Dark Tower II

69

28 May 89*	*The Dark Tower*
	Pet Sematary
	The Dark Tower II
4 Jun 89	*The Dark Tower*
	Pet Sematary
	The Dark Tower II
11 Jun 89	*Pet Sematary*
	The Dark Tower II
18 Jun 89	*The Dark Tower II*
25 Jun 89	*The Dark Tower II*
2 Jul 89	*The Dark Tower*
	The Dark Tower II
9 Jul 89	*The Dark Tower*
	The Dark Tower II
16 Jul 89	*The Dark Tower*
	The Dark Tower II
23 Jul 89	*The Dark Tower*
	The Dark Tower II
30 Jul 89	*The Dark Tower*
	The Dark Tower II
6 Aug 89	*The Dark Tower*
	The Dark Tower II
13 Aug 89	*The Dark Tower*
	The Dark Tower II
20 Aug 89	*The Dark Tower*
	The Dark Tower II
27 Aug 89	*The Dark Tower*
	The Dark Tower II
3 Sep 89	*The Dark Tower II*
10 Sep 89: **None**	
17 Sep 89	*The Dark Tower II*
24 Sep 89	*The Dark Tower II*
1 Oct 89	*The Dark Tower II*

8 Oct 89-29 Oct 89: **None**

5 Nov 89	*The Dark Half*
12 Nov 89	**The Dark Half*
19 Nov 89	**The Dark Half*
26 Nov 89	**The Dark Half*
3 Dec 89	**The Dark Half*
10 Dec 89	**The Dark Half*
17 Dec 89	**The Dark Half*
24 Dec 89	**The Dark Half*

1990

7 Jan 90	**The Dark Half*	*The Dark Tower II*
14 Jan 90	**The Dark Half*	*The Dark Tower II*
21 Jan 90	**The Dark Half*	*The Dark Tower II*
28 Jan 90	*The Dark Half*	*The Dark Tower II*
4 Feb 90*	*The Dark Half*	*The Dark Tower II*
		The Dark Tower
11 Feb 90*	*The Dark Half*	*The Dark Tower II*
		The Dark Tower
18 Feb 90*	*The Dark Half*	*The Dark Tower II*
		The Dark Tower
25 Feb 90	*The Dark Half*	*The Dark Tower*
4 Mar 90: **None**		
11 Mar 90		*The Dark Tower II*

18 Mar 90-6 May 90: **None**

13 May 90	*The Stand: The Complete & Uncut Edition*	
20 May 90	**The Stand: Uncut*	
27 May 90	**The Stand: Uncut*	
3 Jun 90	**The Stand: Uncut*	
10 Jun 90	**The Stand: Uncut*	
17 Jun 90	*The Stand: Uncut*	
24 Jun 90	*The Stand: Uncut*	
1 Jul 90	*The Stand: Uncut*	
8 Jul 90	*The Stand: Uncut*	
15 Jul 90	*The Stand: Uncut*	
22 Jul 90	*The Stand: Uncut*	
29 Jul 90	*The Stand: Uncut*	
5 Aug 90	*The Stand: Uncut*	
12 Aug 90	*The Stand: Uncut*	
19 Aug 90	*The Stand: Uncut*	
26 Aug 90	*The Stand: Uncut*	
2 Sep 90	*The Stand: Uncut*	
9 Sep 90	*The Stand: Uncut*	
16 Sep 90	**Four Past Midnight*	
	The Stand: Uncut	
23 Sep 90*	**Four Past Midnight*	*The Dark Half*
	The Stand: Uncut	
30 Sep 90*	**Four Past Midnight*	**The Dark Half*
	The Stand: Uncut	
7 Oct 90*	**Four Past Midnight*	**The Dark Half*
	The Stand: Uncut	
14 Oct 90*	**Four Past Midnight*	**The Dark Half*
	The Stand: Uncut	

21 Oct 90*	*Four Past Midnight*	***The Dark Half**
	The Stand: Uncut	
28 Oct 90*	*Four Past Midnight*	*The Dark Half*
	The Stand: Uncut	
4 Nov 90*	*Four Past Midnight*	*The Dark Half*
	The Stand: Uncut	
11 No 90	*Four Past Midnight*	*The Dark Half*
18 Nov 90*	*Four Past Midnight*	*The Dark Half* ·
	The Stand: Uncut	
25 Nov 90	*Four Past Midnight*	*The Dark Half*
2 Dec 90*	*Four Past Midnight*	*The Dark Half*
		IT (movie tie-in)
9 Dec 90*	*Four Past Midnight*	*The Dark Half*
		IT
16 Dec 90**	*Four Past Midnight*	*The Dark Half*
		IT
		Misery
23 Dec 90**	*Four Past Midnight*	*The Dark Half*
		IT
		Misery
30 Dec 90**	*Four Past Midnight*	*The Dark Half*
		IT
		Misery

1991

6 Jan 91***	*Four Past Midnight*	***Misery**
	The Stand: Uncut	*IT*
		The Dark Half
13 Jan 91***	*Four Past Midnight*	***Misery**
	The Stand: Uncut	*The Dark Half*
		IT
20 Jan 91**	*Four Past Midnight*	*Misery*
	The Stand: Uncut	*The Dark Half*
27 Jan 91	*Four Past Midnight*	*Misery*
3 Feb 91	*Four Past Midnight*	*Misery*
10 Feb 91	*Four Past Midnight*	*Misery*

17 Feb 91-21 Apr 91: **None**

28 Apr 91		*The Stand: Uncut*
5 May 91		*The Stand: Uncut*
12 May 91		*The Stand: Uncut*
19 May 91		*The Stand: Uncut*
26 May 91		*The Stand: Uncut*
2 Jun 91		*The Stand: Uncut*

9 Jun 91		*The Stand: Uncut*

16 Jun 91-25 Aug 91: **None**

1 Sep 91		*Four Past Midnight*
8 Sep 91		***Four Past Midnight***
15 Sep 91		***Four Past Midnight***
22 Sep 91		*Four Past Midnight*
29 Sep 91		*Four Past Midnight*
6 Oct 91		*Four Past Midnight*
13 Oct 91	*Needful Things*	*Four Past Midnight*
20 Oct 91	*Needful Things*	*Four Past Midnight*
27 Oct 91	*Needful Things*	*Four Past Midnight*
3 Nov 91	*Needful Things*	*Four Past Midnight*
10 Nov 91	*Needful Things*	*Four Past Midnight*
17 Nov 91	*Needful Things*	*Four Past Midnight*
24 Nov 91	*Needful Things*	*Four Past Midnight*
1 Dec 91	*Needful Things*	*Four Past Midnight*
8 Dec 91	*Needful Things*	*Four Past Midnight*
15 Dec 91*	*Needful Things*	*The Dark Tower III: The Waste Lands*
		Four Past Midnight
22 Dec 91*	*Needful Things*	*The Dark Tower III*
		Four Past Midnight
29 Dec 91*	*Needful Things*	*The Dark Tower III*
		Four Past Midnight

1992

5 Jan 92*	*Needful Things*	*The Dark Tower III*
		Four Past Midnight
12 Jan 92	*Needful Things*	*The Dark Tower III*
19 Jan 92	*Needful Things*	*The Dark Tower III*
26 Jan 92	*Needful Things*	*The Dark Tower III*
2 Feb 92	*Needful Things*	*The Dark Tower III*
9 Feb 92	*Needful Things*	*The Dark Tower III*
16 Feb 92	*Needful Things*	*The Dark Tower III*
23 Feb 92	*Needful Things*	*The Dark Tower III*
1 Mar 92		*The Dark Tower III*
8 Mar 92		*The Dark Tower III*

15 Mar 92-21 Jun 92: **None**

28 Jun 92		*Needful Things*
5 Jul 92		*Needful Things*
12 Jul 92	***Gerald's Game***	*Needful Things*

19 Jul 92	*Gerald's Game*	*Needful Things*
26 Jul 92	*Gerald's Game*	*Needful Things*
2 Aug 92	*Gerald's Game*	*Needful Things*
9 Aug 92	*Gerald's Game*	*Needful Things*
16 Aug 92	*Gerald's Game*	*Needful Things*
23 Aug 92	*Gerald's Game*	*Needful Things*
30 Aug 92	*Gerald's Game*	*Needful Things*
6 Sep 92	*Gerald's Game*	*Needful Things*
13 Sep 92	*Gerald's Game*	*Needful Things*
20 Sep 92	*Gerald's Game*	*Needful Things*
27 Sep 92	*Gerald's Game*	*Needful Things*
4 Oct 92	*Gerald's Game*	
11 Oct 92	*Gerald's Game*	
18 Oct 92	*Gerald's Game*	
25 Oct 92	*Gerald's Game*	
1 Nov 92	*Gerald's Game*	
8 Nov 92	*Gerald's Game*	
15 Nov 92	*Gerald's Game*	
22 Nov 92	*Gerald's Game*	
29 Nov 92	*Dolores Claiborne*	
6 Dec 92	**Dolores Claiborne**	
13 Dec 92	**Dolores Claiborne**	***The Dark Tower III***
20 Dec 92	**Dolores Claiborne**	*The Dark Tower III*
27 Dec 92	**Dolores Claiborne**	

1993

3 Jan 93	**Dolores Claiborne**	
10 Jan 93	*Dolores Claiborne*	
17 Jan 93	*Dolores Claiborne*	
23 Jan 93	*Dolores Claiborne*	
31 Jan 93	*Dolores Claiborne*	
7 Feb 93	*Dolores Claiborne*	
14 Feb 93	*Dolores Claiborne*	
21 Feb 93	*Dolores Claiborne*	
28 Feb 93	*Dolores Claiborne*	

7 Mar 93-13 Jun 93: **None**

20 Jun 93		*Gerald's Game*
27 Jun 93		*Gerald's Game*
4 Jul 93		*Gerald's Game*
11 Jul 93		*Gerald's Game*
18 Jul 93		*Gerald's Game*
25 Jul 93		*Gerald's Game*
1 Aug 93		*Gerald's Game*

8 Aug 93		*Gerald's Game*
15 Aug 93		*Gerald's Game*
22 Aug 93		*Gerald's Game*
29 Aug 93		*Gerald's Game*

5 Sep 93-3 Oct 93: **None**

10 Oct 93	*Nightmares & Dreamscapes*	
17 Oct 93	*Nightmares & Dreamscapes*	
24 Oct 93	*Nightmares & Dreamscapes*	
31 Oct 93	*Nightmares & Dreamscapes*	
7 Nov 93	*Nightmares & Dreamscapes*	
14 Nov 93	*Nightmares & Dreamscapes*	
21 Nov 93	*Nightmares & Dreamscapes*	
28 Nov 93	*Nightmares & Dreamscapes*	*Dolores Claiborne*
5 Dec 93	*Nightmares & Dreamscapes*	***Dolores Claiborne***
12 Dec 93	*Nightmares & Dreamscapes*	*Dolores Claiborne*
19 Dec 93	*Nightmares & Dreamscapes*	*Dolores Claiborne*
26 Dec 93	*Nightmares & Dreamscapes*	*Dolores Claiborne*

1994

2 Jan 94	*Nightmares & Dreamscapes*	*Dolores Claiborne*
9 Jan 94	*Nightmares & Dreamscapes*	*Dolores Claiborne*
16 Jan 94	*Nightmares & Dreamscapes*	*Dolores Claiborne*
23 Jan 94	*Nightmares & Dreamscapes*	

30 Jan 94-8 May 94: **None**

15 May 94		*The Stand: Uncut*
22 May 94		***The Stand: Uncut***
29 May 94		*The Stand: Uncut*
5 Jun 94		*The Stand: Uncut*
12 Jun 94		*The Stand: Uncut*

19 Jun 94-7 Aug 94: **None**

14 Aug 94		*Nightmares & Dreamscapes*
21 Aug 94		*Nightmares & Dreamscapes*
28 Aug 94		*Nightmares & Dreamscapes*
4 Sep 94		*Nightmares & Dreamscapes*
12 Sep 94		*Nightmares & Dreamscapes*
19 Sep 94		*Nightmares & Dreamscapes*
26 Sep 94		*Nightmares & Dreamscapes*

2 Oct 94-9 Oct 94: **None**

16 Oct 94	*Insomnia*	
23 Oct 94	*Insomnia*	
30 Oct 94	*Insomnia*	
6 Nov 94	Insomnia	
13 Nov 94	Insomnia	
20 Nov 94	Insomnia	
27 Nov 94	Insomnia	
4 Dec 94	Insomnia	
11 Dec 94	Insomnia	
18 Dec 94	Insomnia	
25 Dec 94	Insomnia	

1995

1 Jan 95	Insomnia	
8 Jan 95	Insomnia	
15 Jan 95	Insomnia	

22 Jan 95-11 Jun 95: **None**

18 Jun 95	Rose Madder	
25 Jun 95	*Rose Madder*	
2 Jul 95	*Rose Madder*	
9 Jul 95	Rose Madder	
16 Jul 95	Rose Madder	
23 Jul 95	Rose Madder	
30 Jul 95	Rose Madder	
6 Aug 95	Rose Madder	
13 Aug 95	Rose Madder	Insomnia
20 Aug 95	Rose Madder	Insomnia
27 Aug 95	Rose Madder	Insomnia
3 Sep 95		Insomnia
10 Sep 95		Insomnia
17 Sep 95		Insomnia
24 Sep 95		Insomnia
1 Oct 95		Insomnia
8 Oct 95		Insomnia

15 Oct 95-31 Dec 95: **None**

1996

7 Jan 96-30 Mar 96: **None**

7 Apr 96	*The Green Mile 1: The Two Dead Girls*

14 Apr 96	*The Green Mile 1*
21 Apr 96	*The Green Mile 1*
28 Apr 96	*The Green Mile 1*
5 May 96	*The Green Mile 2:* *The Mouse on the Mile* *The Green Mile 1*
12 May 96	*The Green Mile 2* *The Green Mile 1*
19 May 96*	*The Green Mile 2* *The Green Mile 1* *Rose Madder*
26 May 96*	*The Green Mile 2* *The Green Mile 1* *Rose Madder*
2 Jun 96**	*The Green Mile 3:* *Coffey's Hands* *The Green Mile 2* *The Greem Mile 1* *Rose Madder*
9 Jun 96**	*The Green Mile 3* *The Green Mile 2* *The Green Mile 1* *Rose Madder*
16 Jun 96**	*The Green Mile 3* *The Green Mile 2* *Rose Madder* *The Green Mile 1*
23 Jun 96**	*The Green Mile 3* *The Green Mile 2* *Rose Madder* *The Green Mile 1*
30 Jun 96**	*The Green Mile 3* *The Green Mile 2* *The Green Mile 1* *Rose Madder*

IV.

KING AND THE CRITICS

To talk about King and critics is tremendously difficult, if only because of the enormous range of statements made about King by critics and about critics by King—to say nothing of King's own contributions to social, cultural, and literary criticism. Each perspective on King results in different possibilities; each works under different (and often mutually exclusive) presuppositions about art and literature; and each addresses radically differing audiences. In this chapter, I have divided an otherwise impossibly cumbersome topic into several more manageable subtopics, beginning with the most accessible and vocal forms of criticism—popular criticism as epitomized by reviews, review-articles, and interviews in daily, weekly, and monthly publications as diverse as the *New York Times Book Review*, the *Kirkus Reviews*, and *The Orange County Register*.

1. Popular Mainstream Criticism

In *The Valley Advocate* for July 21, 1986, Stanley Wiater borrowed the title of this study for an article examining the extent of King's influence and of the increasing critical interest in King. Wiater outlined the three most important directions in King scholarship and criticism to that date: Underwood-Miller's anthologies of essays, *Fear Itself: The Horror Fiction of Stephen King*, *Kingdom of Fear: World of Stephen King*, and a third volume then in preparation; Douglas E. Winter's 1982 *Stephen King* (which he refers to as *The Reader's Guide to Stephen King*) and its subsequent enlargement as *Stephen King: The Art of Darkness* (1984; 1986); and the Starmont series, which he notes is "on a somewhat more 'scholarly' level" than the others. Ostensibly an overview of criticism, Wiater's article serves equally well as an introduction to the difficulty of working with (and writing) King criticism. The article seems oddly schizophrenic, at once inviting and mildly disapproving of such endeavors. While acknowledging that King is a cultural phenomenon, Wiater refers sarcastically to the increasing intensity of critical study: "Yet for the millions of devoted readers who won't leave home without him [King], comes some erudite relief—even more books, not written by King, but about the man and his work." Such books may well become the "next cottage industry in the publishing world," he continues, as they "dissect every corner of the 'Stephen King Phenomenon.'"

Wiater even includes a brief quotation from King relevant to this critical attention. In a tone somewhat moderated from his earlier statements about critics (in the *Adelina* reviews, for example), King defers judgment:

> It's a little bit like Huck Finn and Tom Sawyer going to their own funeral. I'm aware of them. I've read them. For example, Collings' book, *The Many Facets of Stephen King*, which is the latest volume in this parade, has a marvelous and insightful essay on *The Eyes of the Dragon*, which is the children's book that I wrote that will be out in a year or two. That's a good piece. But beyond that, what can I say? They're there, and some of them are good, and some of them are bad, and I'm not going to pick them apart. It's not my place.

Criticism, King concludes, is "their business, not mine. I just write stories."

The article is symptomatic of an attitude that has dogged King's writing from the beginning. At first it was difficult to find neutral—to say nothing of favorable—criticism of King's novels; the concensus seemed to be that any writer who could sell as many books as Stephen King couldn't be worth talking about. By the mid-1980s, when critics began to take him seriously and to explore the complexities of the worlds he creates, they were themselves not taken quite seriously; the prevailing feeling seemed to be that there must be something self-serving in someone who devotes this much time and effort to a writer who is himself "academically" suspect. A decade later, the same attitude persists, in spite of over forty-five secondary books devoted to King, ranging from the *Stephen King Quiz Book* to sophisticated studies by university professor and literary scholars and a 500-page annotated bibliography of things by and about King with a total of more than 5,000 entries.

As a writer, of course, King has confronted this attitude innumerable times. In an interview with Loukia Louka for the *Maryland Coast Dispatch*, when asked how he responds to attacks that he is "not very literary," King answered:

> I don't spend a lot of time worrying about it. If people ask me if I will ever do anything serious, my response is that I'm serious every time I sit down to

write. You decide whether or not what I've done is
serious. I try as hard as I can. It is not really for me
to say or judge what I do. I do the best I can and the
rest of it is up to the critics. Much of it will be decided 50 years after I'm dead. Either the stuff will
still be knocking around or it won't. I think some of
it will be. It might not be taught in upper level English classes. I'm not sure that is its place. But I
think it will be there. Kids will still be checking
'Salem's Lot out of the library. Horror stories have
an incredible staying power.[1]

The comment is apt and appropriate; on the other side of the coin, however, King is not entirely satisfied with commonplace judgments about
himself and his writing. Stephen Beeber asked what King thought
about the fact that for over a decade every novel he published became a
best seller. King replied:

It upsets me in a way sometimes. By being a
bestseller I get the feeling that there's just some kind
of composite of the average American sitting between
my ears, that I fall into the midground of literature—I
guess I'd like to think I'm a little better than that.[2]

Perhaps he is; but he is undoubtedly in a difficult situation as far as
critical reactions go. Since he has chalked up such remarkable commercial successes, it has become almost an article of faith among many
mainstream critics that he is not a writer worth talking about; only
when he distances himself from the kinds of tales that established his
reputation, and embraces politically correct subjects, as in *Gerald's
Game*, does he generally receive approval from those same critics.

During late July and early August, 1986, a number of articles
appeared that discussed two films: *Maximum Overdrive* written and directed by King; and *Stand by Me*, based on "The Body," a novella from
Different Seasons. The reactions to the films aptly define the ambivalent state of King criticism. Associating King's name with a film almost automatically endangers a project, one discovers—a point that
might have been considered more carefully by producers of such subsequent (and frequently aberrant) films as *The Lawnmower Man*, *The
Mangler*, *Stephen King's Graveyard Shift*, and others. Susin Shapiro
focuses on this problem in her "One Picture Is Worth a Million
Words." "No matter what I do," she cites King as saying, "the odds
are good that people are gonna turn around and cream me." In
Shapiro's words, this tendency relates to

...the age-old dilemma of commercial success vs. fine
art; the twain rarely meet. King's brand of kink and
kineticism has brought him a popular success that's
rivaled by very few, but there are killjoys out there
who feel that "mass culture" is a contradiction in
terms. No one is as keenly aware of this as King: in
fact, I've never heard someone so finely attuned to his
own drawbacks, so spot-on about the repercussions of
the limelight.[3]

In a forthright conclusion to the discussion, King talks about his fears
for *The Talisman*, including the sense—later proven reasonably accurate—that critics would savage it because he and Straub were too successful: "When you get too big and too many people like your stuff it
must be mediocre. A mass mind is supposedly ordinary, not sensitive,
literate and smart like the mind of a critic. Of course, it's possible to
dismiss all criticism by saying they're just jealous."[4] He does, however, listen to critics; and he is aware of his faults as a writer—that his
work is derivitive, some of it is simplistic, and that he's not "an original thinker." On the plus side, he attempts to overcome more of these
problems with each new novel.

Still, his understanding and openness did not help when *Maximum Overdrive* was released. It was not just a flawed film, according
to many of the reviews available—it was a *personal* failure for Stephen
King. Larry Ratliff begins his consideration of the film with the confusing assertion that "While it may be some consolation to Stephen
King, this generation's one-man horror gristmill, 'Maximum Overdrive' only proves that the author himself can turn gore into bore just
about as well as more experienced directors." The film is a short story
padded to "an excruciating 97 minutes"; it is a "clunker"; King's
promises to "scare the hell out of us" turn into King "grinding gears
even for his type of audience—the kind who think it's incredibly 'cool'
to watch a movie with feet propped on seats in front of them." The review concludes by comparing *Maximum Overdrive* with the "ultimate
'truck run amok' film," Steven Spielberg's *Duel* (1971), even though
there is little evidence that the two were intended to be compared.[5]

What emerges from the review is not so much an assessment of
a film as an implied critique of Stephen King, of his chosen genre, and
of his status as a best-selling writer.

Robert Garrett begins his discussion of *Maximum Overdrive* by
calling it a "factory reject," its narrative flawed by a "comic book-style
[sic] idiocy that at times is charming." King's debut as a director is
"boneheadedly direct and banal," resulting in a situation that is a "pale
reminder of the beleaguered townies who hid in a diner in 'The Birds,'
although the tiniest of Hitchcock's sparrows is spookier than King's big
wheelers."[6]

It is well and good to compare King's first film to Spielberg and Hitchcock and find it wanting; what Ratliff and Garrett seem to have ignored is King's own assessment of the film. He has frequently called it a "moron movie," meaning that

> ...it isn't a serious picture. You can go to the theater, sit down with a box of popcorn and a drink and believe everything you see for the next two hours. It isn't a serious movie in any way. Just leave your brains outside.[7]

In another response to the "moron film" reference, King simply said:

> This movie is about having a good time at the movies, and that's *all* it's about. Believe me, it's not "My Dinner with Andre." And little Stevie is not rehearsing his Academy Award speech for *this* baby.[8]

The colloquialism of King's comments more than suggest that he did not intend the film to be taken too seriously. Even such disclaimers did not assuage one reviewer, however, who noted that King had called it a "moron movie," but that he had overestimated its effect.

Reactions to *Stand by Me* indicated a parallel strand to King's difficulties. The film was superbly directed by Rob Reiner, who made several changes in King's original narrative, even commenting that "Stephen's novella was set in 1960, but since I was twelve in 1959, we moved it back a year, because the references seemed even more natural to me. The film became a blend of Stephen's story and mine.... The film only came into focus after I made my own personal connections to it."[9] The screenplay was written by Raynold Gideon and Bruce A. Evans, who, with Andrew Scheinman, also produced the film.

King's contribution to *Stand by Me* was thus diluted as the material passed through several hands; in fact, it seems probable that King's connections with the original narrative were purposely downplayed—a treatment similar to Frank Darabont's remarkable transformation of "Rita Hayworth and Shawshank Redemption" into an Academy Award winning film. Daniel Cziraky notes that "as bankable as King's name has become in the publishing world, the poor performance of past films based on his works was most likely a very big factor in Columbia's releasing the film as 'Stand by Me,' 'A Rob Reiner Film,' instead of Stephen King's 'The Body.'"[10] While such thinking might be logical, Cziraky writes, it has the unfortunate side effect of distancing King from the finest film adaptation of his works yet produced.

In spite of that distancing, however, a number of reviewers seem intent on bringing King into the discussion. Generally speaking, according to several early reviewers, where the film succeeds it shows Reiner's hand; where it fails, it shows King's. Rex Reed disliked the film, noting that "rarely have 90 minutes of screen time been devoted to anything more trivial or pointless." He carefully includes the comment that the film was based on a story by King, "who publishes everything but his grocery list and calls it literature....,"[11] a comment that may have some validity in terms of King's reputation as a writer, but seems to have little direct bearing on a film several stages removed from King's prose. The implication is that the film is suspect simply because of its relation to Stephen King. Kevin Lally finds the film much stronger, a "delightful sleeper," a "raucously appealing portrait of 12-year-olds." Yet he also insists that the underlying narrative is atypical of King, improved by strong directing by Reiner and equally strong writing by Gideon and Evans. Overall, the review is positive and helpful—until Lally feels it necessary to discuss King directly. *Stand by Me* is told from the point of view of Gordon Lachance, a successful writer:

> But if Gordie is meant to be King's alter ego, his pensive style gives no clue that it belongs to someone who's made his fortune from pulpy, grundgy horror stories.
> Still, the one yarn young Gordie tells his friends—about a fat boy's disgusting revenge on his hometown—is in tune with the King that America has taken to heart.[12]

King's novella might have seemed to portray Lachance as "King's alter ego," particularly since the two stories interpolated into "The Body" were in fact juvenilia by King; he is himself aware of the suggested connection, as is evidenced by a comment in a letter discussing *IT* that "Derry is no more Bangor than Gordie Lachance is the young Steve King."[13]

Stand by Me is even less transparent in this regard than was "The Body." The film's Gordie seems to reflect Rob Reiner as much Stephen King: "The feelings Gordie expresses in the film were very much like the feelings I've had for most of my life," Reiner said in an interview.[14] Lally's attempt to find King within the film, and subsequently to use that discovery as a springboard for a negative statement about King's writing career, seems unfair to King, to Reiner, and to the film.

Richard Freedman uses the same technique in his review: the film is strong because of Reiner, weak when it depends on King's narrative. "Considering what a disaster Stephen King's 'Maximum Overdrive' is," Freedman begins,

...directed by the best-selling horror novelist himself, it's a pleasure to report that "Stand by Me," based on his novella "The Body," is an almost unqualified success.

But then it's directed by Rob Reiner as skilled behind the camera as King is a seemingly hopeless duffer.

Later, Freedman details several weaknesses in the film:

Poorest of all, there's a kind of pity and self-aggrandizement on the part of the author that nearly spoils the tone of this dark idyl:

"You're going to be a great writer some day, Gordie," Chris tells him, and one can just see King licking his chops as he set that line down (actually, in all fairness, the screen adaptation is by co-producers Raynold Gideon and Bruce A. Evans, but would Tolstoy have been capable of such self-preening fatuity?)[15]

The parenthetical comment is itself confusing, since it seems at once to accuse King and to expiate him—and why the reference to Tolstoy in the first place? Nor, in the context of the film, is Chris's line out of place. Gordie has just admitted his deepest fears—that his father hates him, that he is no good—and Chris comforts him by admiring the one talent the film has clearly established that Gordie possesses: his ability to tell stories. At least three time prior to this scene, Chris has complimented Gordie on that skill; what better way to build up the younger boy's shattered self-image. To charge King with intruding "pity and self-aggrandizement" into the film works against the nature of *Stand by Me*.

The film is strong—ranking with *The Dead Zone, The Woman in the Room*, and *The Shawshank Redemption* among the most successful King adaptations, with a fine screenplay and sensitive, careful directing. But to remove King from the equation entirely is as unfair as to blame him for every infelicity in the film. Yet many of the strongest responses to *Stand by Me* did precisely that.

Sheila Benson wrote in the *Los Angeles Times* that the film was the "summer's great gift, a compassionate perfectly formed look at the real heart of youth." She commends the writers, the actors, and especially the director; Reiner "has seen that the cast stays honest and his movie marvelously restrained."[16] There is no mention at all of Stephen King.

Tom Cuneff does refer to King, but in the opening sentence, and then by way of establishing one condition for the film's success:

"Though this movie is based on a novella...by scaremeister Stephen King, it's not just another one of his chillers."[17] The remainder of the review is perceptive and positive, but ignores King.

Similarly, David Brooks's review concentrates on Reiner, on the narrative, on the actors, and on the relationships among the characters, but mentions King only once, in a paragraph that sounds a familiar chord: "Who could have predicted that a movie, let alone a very good movie, could be made from a story about four 12-year-olds hiking to find a dead boy? Set in 1959 and based on Stephen King's novella 'The Body,' 'Stand by Me' is an author's remembrance of his pivotal childhood adventure."[18] The author in question is not even King; Brooks's next sentence speaks of Gordie Lachance, not Stephen King.

In the cases of *Maximum Overdrive* and *Stand by Me*, King's reputation is an almost impossible barrier to overcome. One film apparently failed because of King; the second succeeded in spite of him. Nor has the situation changed substantially in ten years. When *The Shawshank Redemption* appeared, some viewers expressed astonishment when they learned that it was taken from a King story. Certainly Frank Darabont deserves all of the credit he has received for recognizing and encapsulating the original story's strengths (and for struggling for years to make the film), but critical reactions nonetheless still tend to follow the lines established by Reiner's success with *Stand by Me*.

The situation with King criticism in general] is equally diverse. In "King of Horror," Robert Hunt prefaces his discussion of film adaptations by arguing that

> King is the Steven Spielberg of horror. Like Spielberg, he's obsessed with popular culture, and particularly with those parts of it which he grew up watching: King would like to believe that his taste and sensibility have remained unchanged since the seventh grade. No pop culture revisionist, King deals with horror archetypes: if he writes about a vampire, you can be sure he won't leave out the coffin, the stake, or the garlic; his werewolf, likewise, will be destroyed only by a silver bullet during a full moon. But King also recognizes that his subjects are archetypal, and knows just how much distance to keep from them. He knows his horror traditions, and knows better than to take them too seriously.[19]

Yet Hunt follows this paragraph with the disclaimer that he is referring only to the plots in the film adaptations; he has read few of King's novels, he admits, and those were "uninteresting stylistically." *Carrie* was a pot-boiler, a "routine entry in the then popular cycle of books about possessed kids"; *Cujo* is silly, and *Christine* even sillier, with the film's few impressive moments the result of John Carpenter moving away from King's "hot-rod version of *Carrie*" toward an emphasis on human characters. *Cat's Eye* succeeds better than did *Creepshow*, although largely because the later film is "perhaps the sort of thing that King...does best: simple, slightly familiar suspense situations that don't take themselves too seriously."[20] The point of Hunt's extensive analyses seems to be that the films are superior to the novels; yet even in discussing the films, Hunt carefully identifies King's failings as a writer.

Many reviews of King's novels have paralleled these attitudes. *Kirkus Reviews* (August 15, 1975) referred to *'Salem's Lot* as "super-exorcism that leaves the taste of somebody else's blood in your mouth and what a bad taste it is.... Vampirism, necrophilia, *et* dreadful *alia* rather overplayed...."

Jack Sullivan's "Ten Ways to Write a Gothic" takes King severely to task for stylistic blunders: "To say Stephen King is not an elegant writer...is putting it mildly." He particularly dislikes King's use of parentheses, capitals, and exclamation marks as points of emphasis in *The Shining*: "Sometimes non-punctuation or italics are used—quite arbitrarily—for gimmicky stream of consciousness effect." In addition, the novel's plot is obviously a reworking of Poe, Blackwood, and Lovecraft, as well as such films as *Diabolique*, *Psycho*, and the *Village of the Damned*; perhaps Sullivan might have discussed such internal referents as "allusions" in another writer, but for some reason, King is not allowed the liberty of building on the literary past, even though he acknowledges his debt to that past throughout the novel.[21]

Michael Mewshaw similar attacked King as stylist in "Novels and Stories," which also appeared in the *New York Times Book Review* (March 26, 1978). The *Night Shift* stories may be imaginative, but they suffer from "twist endings that should have died with O. Henry, the hoariest clichés of the horror-tale subgenre...and lines that provoke smiles rather than terror."[22]

Eight years later, King's most ambitious novel has come in for a similar drubbing. John Podhoretz's review of *IT* is written as a parody of the novel itself, with four parts and a narrative tone and style clearly based on King's own:

> *It can't be, it just can't be*, he thought wildly, *not again, not SO SOON*! He was quaking in his Nocona boots. For there, sitting right there, as though God or the devil
> (*it's the latter oh God it's the latter oh I know it's the devil*)

had placed it there, was a gigantic book with a dark painting on the cover, and in large red type, the word "It."[23]

The parody continues in this vein, criticizing the novel (as King had predicted) for its length: 1,138 pages (the 1978 hardcover of *The Stand* was only 823 pages long, with the 1990 *Complete & Uncut Edition* topping *IT*'s length by only fifteen pages). As early as the *Adelina* reviews, King noted that as far as mainstream critics were concerned, the long novel had died long ago, and that since the 1950s, novels were more and more frequently discriminated against on the basis of length alone. "Many critics," he noted in 1980, "seem to take a novel of more than 400 pages as a personal affront." As evidence, he cites negative responses to *The Dead Zone* ("One critic was so put out by [its] length...that he wished I might contract a case of permanent dyslexia") and *The Stand* (King cites one comment to the effect that "Given enough rope, any writer will hang himself...and in this novel, King has taken enough rope to outfit an entire clipper ship").[24]

It was not surprising, then, that King would anticipate even more negative responses to *IT* largely on the basis of its length. In one letter, he noted sadly that "the days when *any* novel as long as this gets much of a critical reading are gone."[25] In a lighter vein, he acknowledged the difficulty of reading such a massive work. After seeing the entire manuscript in a single stack, he writes, "a Great Postulate occurred to me: no manuscript weighing more than twelve pounds can *possibly* be any good. I also made my first New Year's Resolution in some ten years that night: *Never write anything bigger than your own head.*"[26]

King was, therefore, prepared to some extent for reactions such as Podhoretz's to *IT*, at least as far as the novel's length is concerned.

Podhoretz found more to quibble with in the novel than mere length, however. *IT* demonstrates all of King's trademarks: a setting in Maine; quotations from rock songs; blood and gore; brand names; geographical accuracy to tie its horrors to the real world; "real get-down-in-the-gutter-and-sound-like-an-illiterate-moron-writing" set next to passages of more self-consciously elevated prose. The latter criticism sounds much like Mark Twain's condemnation of James Fenimore Cooper's literary offenses.

In despair, Podhoretz consults his own Von Helsing, a certain Dr. Smith, a mild-mannered University English professor by day and researcher into the occult by night. Smith warns Podhoretz that King must be stopped: "If you don't, this will go on forever. He'll publish longer and longer books. Two, three thousand pages. Five thousand. Your life will be devoted to reading his books. You will quit your job, you'll have no money, and you'll starve to death."

The result is a quick trip to Maine, where Podhoretz confronts King to define the ultimate failure of *IT*—it is boring. It depends upon the banality of blood, upon extensive passages of cruelty to create the interest that its implicit horror-elements cannot. King is no longer scary, Podhoretz asserts, so he had to fall back on unpleasantness (apparently ignoring King's claims that unpleasantness—what King refers to as the "gross out"—is inherent in King's theory of horror).

Not that King was always such, Podhoretz adds; once, in fact, he was a master of sorts—but Podhoretz carefully undercuts the positive with the negative. *The Stand* was a great novel, he says, adding the derogatory "in its own pulpy way":

> "The Shining" was genuinely imaginative and "'Salem's Lot" the only vampire novel worthy of comparison to "Dracula."
> But now where are you? You're hoping that prolixity will accomplish what your imagination can't.[27]

With *IT*, King has given up on the supernatural and hopes to frighten by sheer bulk and page count. The novel is boring, King is boring, and Podhoretz warns that if this sort of thing continues, King will lose his fans.

There are, of course, positive reviews of *IT*—many of them. But even there, a certain oddly lingering reticence attaches itself, often in unusual ways. *The Los Angeles Times Book Review* included a strongly favorable piece on the novel:

> I wait for each new King novel as an alcoholic waits for the next drink. I am addicted. If you are not, I suggest you introduce yourself to King's work through one of his earlier novels—"Carrie" or "The Shining." If, however, you are already a King addict, "It" will overwhelm you.[28]

The difficulty lies not so much in what is said (although the review is essentially plot summary rather than evaluation) as in who says it: Whoopi Goldberg, whose listed credentials are restricted to her work in film and theater. While she certainly has a right to an attitude toward King and King's novels, it unfortunately seems possible that her assignment to review the book was as much a mark of her reputation as a Hollywood personality as of her literary expertise.

This emphasis on personality leads to another form of popular criticism, which tends to ignore the works themselves and concentrate on *King* as personality—generally to his detriment. For one writer, what seems most important is King's "long lantern-jawed face framed by a jet black bowl of hair that rises in two sweeping arcs around his forehead like the drooping wings of some bat"[29] (Beeber 16A); for yet another, it is the hamburger he eats on the set of *Maximum Overdrive*, a greasy hamburger dripping with blood-like catsup.

The problem is, of course, that it is difficult to see exactly what his hamburger or hairstyle have to do with the quality of his writing or directing—and yet they are treated as if they were of paramount importance. John Coyne was speaking of this sort of pseudo-criticism, criticism by personality, when he commented that King was becoming his "own worst enemy"—Stephen King the writer was being replaced by Stephen King the visible personality. "You really shouldn't be known," Coyne says.

> J. D. Salinger has probably sold a lot more copies just because no one knows who J. D. Salinger is. If King or I wanted to play this game really well, we would be totally anonymous. We would be sending books in via UPS. King's problem—and it's a problem for all of us—is, what if he wants to write a love story? If he writes under his own name, he'll disappoint his readers, because they're expecting, if nothing else, that one lover will chop off the other's head or whatever.[30]

In King's case, it has progressed even beyond that sort of disappointment. Now, a novel or film must live up to the media hype, *and* up to the popular image of King himself as the "titan of terror" and the "king of horror," *and* up to the impossible expectations generated by over fifty books and twenty-five film adaptations in just over twenty years.

Paradoxically, because of his popular and commercial successes it becomes more and more difficult for King to attain critical success.

2. Academic Criticism

Thus far, I have concentrated only on one sort of criticism—what might be called mainstream, non-academic, and popular criticism—and one sort of reaction to King.

There are, of course, others.

Academic critics have discovered King and are in many cases working diligently to place King within the framework of an acknowledged traditional literary heritage. In spite of references to such critical and scholarly endeavors as fostering a "cottage industry," anthologies of essays, such as Darrell Schweitzer's *Discovering Stephen King* (1985) and Underwood and Miller's *Fear Itself: The Horror Fiction of Stephen King* (1982; 1984) and *Kingdom of Fear: The World of Stephen*

King (1986), include a number of valuable studies. One particularly useful piece, Michael McDowell's "The Unexpected and the Inevitable," begins by disparaging the "sapping methods of literary 'appreciation' taught in colleges and graduate schools," then proceeds to demonstrate graphically and convincingly King's mastery of pacing and rhythm. McDowell's chapter in *Kingdom of Fear* not only elucidates an important element in King's appeal to readers, but simultaneously provides an example of literary criticism that makes a difference for the readers.

Other articles on King have found their ways into periodicals—scholarly and academic journals not devoted to King studies or even to horror literature. James Egan's 1986 essay, "'A Single Powerful Spectacle': Stephen King's Gothic Melodrama," concentrates on King's relationship to a literary thread extending from Mary Shelley through Bram Stoker, Henry James, and Shirley Jackson, concluding that "King's treatment of the Gothic and the macabre are the opposite of impulsive meanderings—he consistently seeks to create a 'single powerful spectacle'" within a tradition that "has existed from the beginnings of literary history."[31] Two years earlier, Egan published "Apocalypticism in the Fiction of Stephen King," also in *Extrapolation*; in the same year *Clues: A Journal of Detection* published his "Antidetection: Gothic and Detective Conventions in the Fiction of Stephen King." In 1986, Gary William Crawford's new journal *Gothic* published Kenneth Gibbs's "Stephen King and the Tradition of American Gothic," a study of King in the context not only of Stoker, Poe, James, and Hawthorne, but also of Herman Melville. Karen McGuire's "The Artist as Demon in Mary Shelley, Stevenson, Walpole, Stoker, and King," including an extensive discussion of Ben Mears in *'Salem's Lot*, appeared in the same issue.

Since that time, the number of academic or scholarly treatments of King's works has increased dramatically. Book-length studies now include *The Gothic World of Stephen King: Landscapes of Nightmares*, edited by Gary Hoppenstand and Ray B. Browne (1987); *Stephen King: The First Decade,* by Joseph Reino (1988); *Landscape of Fear*, by Tony Magistrale (1988); *The Unseen King,* by Tyson Blue (1989); *The Stephen King Companion* (1989, revised edition, 1995), edited by George Beahm, and *The Stephen King Story* (1991), by Beahm; *The Moral Voyages of Stephen King*, by Anthony Magistrale (1989); *Stephen King: Man and Artist*, by King's former teacher and recognized literary scholar, Carroll F. Terrell (1990); *The Shining Reader*, edited by Anthony Magistrale (1991); *The Shape Under the Sheet: The Complete Stephen King Encyclopedia*, edited by Stephen Spignesi (1991); *The Dark Descent: Essays Defining Stephen King's Horrorscape*, edited by Tony Magistrale (1992); *Stephen King: The Second Decade,* Danse Macabre *to* The Dark Half, by Tony Magistrale (1992); *A Casebook on* The Stand, edited by Tony Magistrale (1992);

Stephen King's America, by Jonathan P. Davis (1994); *Stephen King*, by Amy Keyishian and Marjorie Keyishian (1995); and *The Work of Stephen King*, by Michael R. Collings (1996). Several of these have appeared from University Presses; others are the work of scholars well skilled in the art and craft of literary discourse.

This listing of titles is not to argue, however, that King has reached universal academic "respectability" as yet—or even that he wishes to do so. There are sufficient reactions to scholarly articles on King as fostering a "cottage industry," and to "instant criticism," that suggest academe still views the man and his critics with a jaundiced eye.

Gary K. Wolfe's review-article in *Modern Fiction Studies*, for example, attempted an overview of recent scholarship in science fiction and fantasy. The pages devoted to King criticism argue that Winter's *Stephen King: The Art of Darkness* is the "only book on Stephen King anyone really needs."32 The comment sets aside the fact that Winter's book is admittedly more of an appreciation than a critical or scholarly approach to King; in spite of its many excellences, it lacks a certain balance of perception and occasionally overstates its arguments. Gary William Crawford, for instance, concludes his own critical overview of horror and the literature of the supernatural by noting that King has been the object of several studies, including Winter's. Winter's book is sound," Crawford argues, "but one would think from reading it that King is another Shakespeare; his praise is unqualified.33

Still, what is most frustrating about Wolfe's essay is not his singling out an individual volume, but his general attitude toward King and King criticism as a whole. The essay approaches its stated subject, science fiction and fantasy, with a certain seriousness of tone that does Wolfe justice; certainly his discussions of the backgrounds to SF criticism and of such eminent figures in the field as Thomas Clareson, J. G. Ballard, and Philip José Farmer are carefully constructed and effectively argued. Only with King does Wolfe allow the level of his discourse to alter. "As everyone knows," Wolfe writes,

> ...there are eight hundred zillion copies of King's books in print, which if lined up end-to-end would free up a considerable amount of shelf space in your local B. Dalton's.34

Later, in discussing the Starmont series, Wolfe uses such phrases as "flush on the heels of what must have been its greatest success," to comment that Starmont is "brandishing at us not one or two but *seven* more books about Stephen King!" On the basis of three, Wolfe feels able to comment on the entire series—and states so specifically.

The difficulty here is that almost everything related to King and horror fiction is treated with an entirely different tone than that which characterizes the rest of the essay. Colloquialisms, exaggerations, exclamations, italicized phrases suggest an underlying attitude not only toward the critics and their writings but toward King himself.

The uncomfortable fact is that King criticism is occasionally as suspect among academics as King's novels are. Certainly that is not the case everywhere; and equally certainly much of the academic establishment's antagonism toward King is softening. Yet the fact remains that many academic writers do not read King, have never read King, and have no inclination to ever read King—much less spend time on critical studies.

On the more positive side, King has participated in scholarly conferences, notably the fifth International Conference on the Fantastic in the Arts, held at Boca Raton, Florida, March 22-25, 1984. King served as guest of honor, delivering a lecture later published in *Fantasy Review* as "Dr. Seuss and the Two Faces of Fantasy."[35] Even more noteworthy for this discussion, he was the subject of a double session of academic papers chaired by Leonard G. Heldreth of Northern Michigan University at Marquette. The papers presented included "Stephen King's Vietnam Allegory: An Interpretation of 'Children of the Corn,'" by Tony Magistrale of the University of Vermont, Burlington; "The Destruction and Re-Creation of the Human Community in Stephen King's *The Stand*," by Burton Hatlen, King's former professor at the University of Maine at Orono; "Stephen King's *The Stand*: Science Fiction into Fantasy," by Michael R. Collings of Pepperdine University; "Strawberry Spring: Stephen King's Gothic Universe," by Mary Ferguson of the University of Georgia, Athens; and "Monster Love; or, Why Is Stephen King?" by Dennis O'Donovan of Florida Atlantic University. Several of the presentations were subsequently published; at least one first appeared in a scholarly quarterly and was then reprinted in a small-press fan publication. In general, the responses to King at this session indicate the range and scope of the more positive academic responses to his work.

Finally, in terms of serious literary responses to King, the Starmont series attempted to indicate some possibilities for King criticism. Beginning with *Discovering Stephen King* and *Stephen King as Richard Bachman* (1985) and running through Tony Magistrale's *A Casebook on The Stand* (1992), each volume explored facets of King's works: pseudonymous novels, short stories, novels, films produced from King's fictions, and occasionally extra-literary considerations in dealing with King and his reputation, his relation to the culture and climate of late twentieth-century America, his impact on publishing and on popular literature. The volumes were not all specifically academic; many were, instead, intended for serious readers of King who might benefit from discussions, backgrounds, and generalized analysis. In addition, they tried to bridge the often too-apparent gap between academic criticism and general readership by approaching King from two directions: first, by showing that the standards of traditional and contemporary literary criticism might be justifiably and beneficially applied to King's writings; and second, by showing readers that some familiarity with those standards may be helpful in appreciating and understanding more fully King's achievements.

3. Criticism Within the Genre: Appreciations, Peer Criticism, and Fan Responses

On yet another level, some readers respond to King's stories with personal, gut reactions, often displaying unallayed adoration—one fan referred to the "orgasmic" experience of reading King's novels. Among fans, for example, criticism emphasizes what the individual reader felt while immersed in the works; there is in general less concern for establishing literary criteria for success or failure.

Paradoxically, Winter's *Stephen King: The Art of Darkness* to a degree falls within this category, since it is an appreciation and biography, coupled with literary criticism that emphasizes psychology and symbolism as well as King's own background. Winter's study has been justifiably influential in interesting readers and writers in King; much of the secondary work done since 1982 depends upon questions Winter posed, evaluations he made, assertions he brought forth. The book represents a fine blend of the fan and the academic, although given Winter's credits as a contributing editor for *Fantasy Review* he might lean more toward fan than academic.

Unfortunately, the dichotomy perceived by many as existing between fan response and academic criticism is rarely so neatly resolved. In an intriguing article published in *Castle Rock: The Stephen King Newsletter*, Christopher Spruce seemed intent on tackling the arbitrary definition of "literature" as "whatever college students study in literature classes, the works having been so deemed by a panel of self-appointed literary experts—usually college professors."[36] Placing King in the context of contemporary American writers, including John Irving, Norman Mailer, and John Updike, Spruce wonders why King is simply disregarded as a writer of horror pulps who has committed the worst possible crime: he sells too many books.

Spruce's discussion is clear up to the point where he refers to those King works that he would nominate as true "literature": "The Reach" and *'Salem's Lot*. His judgment is not particularly the issue here; both are strong works, and "The Reach" does touch on important archetypal and mythic chords. The difficulty is that, after carefully breaking down the barriers separating King from "good literature," the article then evaluates these two works from a rather fannish perspective. The discussion of "The Reach" concentrates on plot summary and personal response; Spruce empathizes with Stella Flanders because she reminds him of many elderly women he has known in Maine and because she represents a certain sort of character that appeals to him. "Beyond that," he writes in the final paragraph devoted to the story, "my literary senses tell me that this is as good a story as I probably am ever going to have the pleasure of reading."[37]

What is missing is a clear discussion of *why* the story succeeds, not only as entertainment but as literature. And that is the point missing in many fan responses. Adulation is there, but without careful discussion and definition of relevant literary criteria; what is there besides the reader's "literary senses" that demonstrates King's mastery of language and form. Frequently, responses at this level concentrate on story line and on the sensation of fear King's stories and novels produce. These are certainly valid responses (and just as certainly not the only ones possible). The many appreciations, reviews, letters, and informal articles published in *Castle Rock: The Stephen King Newsletter*, for example, go far toward establishing the extent of King's popularity and the depth to which his works are capable of touching readers, regardless of the opinions of mainstream reviewers or academic critics.

As in so many other ways, King remains controversial when it comes to critics and criticism. This chapter represents only an overview of possibilities; it does not pretend to a definitive treatment of the issue. *The Work of Stephen King: An Annotated Bibliography and Guide* (1996) lists several hundred secondary works relating to King and his writing; each approaches the subject from a different critical and personal stance; each illuminates a slightly different perspective on the man and his works; and each defines for itself the importance—or lack of importance—King holds in contemporary American culture.

V.

KING AND THE SCHOOLMASTERS: A PERSONAL PERSPECTIVE[1]

Several years ago, my then-teenage second son came home chuckling from a trying day in high school; his attitude was in itself an odd enough circumstance to merit remembering. But the reason for his laughter was even more intriguing than the fact of it, particularly since it bore directly on my own work in Science Fiction, Fantasy, and Horror criticism—and specifically with Stephen King criticism.

His junior English class was preparing to face the great unmentionable, the terror of the year—the dreaded TERM PAPER, the only long research paper he would be expected (forced?) to write during what he considered his four years' internment in high school. His teacher had handed out a long list of American authors judged suitable as topics for a researched paper and had instructed the students to submit proposals for a paper that would discuss at least three works by a single author, or one work by three authors. Of course, they would also be responsible for locating a number of appropriate outside sources as well.

During the discussion, one student (not my son) noted aloud that his favorite author, Stephen King, was not on the list.

"No," the teacher responded solemnly, King was not on the list.

Another student noted that several other contemporary popular writers were also missing from the list.

"Yes," the teacher said, they were missing, since such writers were only of interest to readers unable to handle the sophisticated expression of the "classics."

"In other words," the second student shot back, defending himself and his friends who read King and the other "unmentionables," "we read them because we're too stupid to understand the classics?"

"Uh, no," the teacher answered, obviously backpedaling. She continued to talk in generalities about the lack of sophistication in contemporary popular writers, noting that most students hadn't even considered using King as a topic for the paper until a few years earlier, when a professor from Pepperdine began publishing books about him.

At this point, my son sat up and began paying closer attention.

Then, the teacher continued, the professor made the situation worse by holding discussion groups at the local library, actually talking with groups of high-school students about King and his works as if they had literary merit.

Now my son was *really* paying attention, wondering if he should raise his hand and say "That was my father," or wait it out and see what else would be said.

He decided to wait it out.

And in doing so, he discovered to his surprise that in spite of such decidedly odd behavior for a college professor as writing *books* about Stephen King (fortunately apparently isolated to this single aberration), there really wasn't enough criticism on King or writers like him to merit including them on the list of possible topics for the Term Paper.

.   End of discussion.

When my son reported this experience—grinning the whole while and (I'm sure) wondering how I would take the implied slur on my academic reputation (such as it is)—I was struck again by the short-sightedness of academic establishments that continue to exclude King and others like him from lists of "approved" materials.

On the one hand, while Hawthorne and *The Scarlet Letter*, Melville and *Moby Dick*, and Dickens and *A Tale of Two Cities* are certainly significant literary achievements in our culture, no doubt fascinating topics for further research and discussion by adult readers and scholars, I am even less convinced now than I was as a high-school student that they are necessarily appropriate for freshmen, sophomores, and juniors in high school, many if not most of whom are barely beyond being functionally literate, many of whom lack even the barest backgrounds or historical perspectives for assessing such novels, and many of whom are explicitly more interested in Poe, Bradbury, and King than in any of the classics. Yet many instructors are forced in turn by district policies to force high-school students to read works that probably even most teachers would be unlikely to read for pleasure.

On the other hand, the opposite alternative seems to be to require texts that are themselves less literary expressions than exercises in staid political correctness, sociological conditioning, and artificially induced diversity. Either way, the established programs often simply ignore the fact that students often don't like to read much voluntarily, but a great many of them *do* like to read (and even watch) things by Stephen King.

There are, of course, strong arguments against allowing King into curriculums, particularly at the high school level, even on as tangentially a basis as letting students use his works for an out-of-class term paper.

His writing is often violent.

96

It is often gross and explicit, both sexually and linguistically.

It is often fantastic it uncomfortable ways.

It is often highly critical of accepted institutions, including home, family, politics, religion, and education.

His books are challenging to students and to adults, to the extent that "The Most Frequently Banned Books in the 1990s,"[2] an online discussion of censorship, included *Christine* and *Cujo* in the top fifty banned children's books (along with such titles as *The Adventures of Huckleberry Finn*, Katherine Paterson's *The Bridge to Terebithia*, Madeleine L'Engle's *A Wrinkle in Time*, and Jacob and Wilhelm Grimm's "Little Red Riding-Hood"—on the whole, rather nice company for King's books to share). At one time or another, almost all of King's books have been challenged as being decidedly inappropriate for student readers.

But students *read* his books. Based on those experiences leading discussion groups about his books at the local library, it became clear to me that high-school-ages readers often *devour* his books, memorize his books, know more about what he has written than I do. At the discussion groups, held over the span of five or six years, audiences of seventy-five to one hundred high-school students (and occasionally teachers and parents) gathered to talk about specific King novels, and they immediately demonstrated that the majority of them had not only read the book assigned but a number of other titles as well. When I substituted for an ailing discussion leader and attempted to work with another text, one more mainstream and more recognizably a "classic," the group shrank to less than fifty, only a handful of whom had ever read anything by the author in question (to say nothing of the book under discussion), and even fewer of whom evinced any inclination to talk about the novel or its author.

But students *do* read Stephen King.

And then they are told by many teachers that he is too unsophisticated, too peripheral to what is really important in the universe, too *common* for students to waste their time on, when it would seem that teachers would welcome the opportunity to confront a writer who perhaps more than any other is molding the imaginations and minds of contemporary adolescents. After all, if so many students read him, and he is so awful, so damaging to the social fabric, so utterly without redeeming social value, it would seem even more important to discover what it is that draws young readers to him. To refer back to my son's experience, the teacher stated to the class that anyone who read more than two or three King novels had to be warped, perverted, highly disturbed. At that point my son couldn't help laughing out loud—and was tempted to put the teacher even more on the spot by noting that he (my son) had read about thirty King novels and that his father had read *everything* that King had published. If reading two or three books relegated a reader to *warp*-dom, where would thirty, forty, or fifty books put someone? Perhaps wisely, my son restrained his impulse, and the teacher was free to continue her defense of the *status quo* reading list.

No, King is not sufficiently elevated, not sufficiently elegant, not sufficiently a part of most teachers' own academic backgrounds (implying that they might actually have to read him and study him themselves in order to lecture to classes) to be considered appropriate as the subject for a research project.

And to prove their point, many high-school and occasionally even college teachers pound the final nail into the coffin of any would-be term-paperist: *There's just not enough criticism written about him to make the effort worthwhile.*

Again and again I have heard this comment and been stunned at the ignorance it betrays. Certainly for many Science Fiction, Fantasy, and Horror writers, the claim is accurate. Even some of the finest writers in the genres have been ignored by traditional critics and scholars, to the point that accurate bibliographies are not even available for many, if not most. In spite of the valiant efforts of publishers like the late Ted Dikty of Starmont House and his series editor, Roger C. Schlobin, who between the two of them saw to the publication of several dozen introductory monographs; or Rob Reginald at Borgo Press, with his continuing series of definitive bibliographies; or the Greenwood Press monographs on Science Fiction and Fantasy—in spite of the work of dozens of scholars and critics approaching such monumental tasks as the life works of Isaac Asimov and Robert A. Heinlein and others almost as prolific and as central to our reading heritage—in spite of all of this effort, it is still too easy for teachers to issue lists of term-paper topics that ignore some of the most popular and, more critically, some of the most influential writers of our times.

But to make that claim for Stephen King?

I glance at my bookshelf and see the one-and-one-half-inch-thick book that represents my work on a Stephen King bibliography, *The Work of Stephen King*, and I wonder. After four updatings, what began as *The Annotated Guide to Stephen King* (1986) now covers almost 500 pages and includes over *5,000* items, both primary and secondary, including titles of several dozen books exclusively about King (a number of them from prestigious university presses); more dozens of articles in scholarly and popular journals and magazines; hundreds of reviews ranging from the *New York Times Book Review* to localized fan presses; and articles in newspapers, newsletters, and assorted other print, audio, and video media—but this abundance seems not enough to allow students sufficient exercise in the fine and ancient art of literary research.

Granted, not all of the criticism and scholarship available on King is first class. I think of one article that discovers Vietnam allegories in a King story, when King himself has stated publicly that he sees (or intended) no such subtext himself. Or another critic who, after publishing three very expensive specialty editions of interviews and criticism, notes that he considers King little more than a literary hack (although presumably a source of no insignificant income). Many of the articles and some of the books contain little more than whole-hearted appreciations by energetic and occasionally ecstatic fans.

Nevertheless, it seems important to recognize that much of the criticism is solid, and, more important yet, that horror writers are an intrinsic and essential part of understanding late twentieth-century American culture. Writers like Stephen King, Dean Koontz, Robert McCammon, Dan Simmons, and others have published works that transcend narrow genre classifications, that grapple with fundamental social problems we face today and explore them through *metaphors* of the monstrous and the horrific—as if AIDS, molestation, homelessness, and the damaging *-isms* of various sorts that infect our world were not already monstrous and horrific enough. These writers have described *us* in the clearest and broadest of terms, not pessimistically or nihilistically but often with an undercurrent of true hope. On the surface, their images may be frightening, but then so is our world. The "pre-millennial cotillion" that Koontz depicts graphically in *Dragon Tears*, for example, is not just a figment of his imagination, nor is the corruption endemic to *Dark Rivers of the Heart*, nor the horrifyingly dispassionate cruelty at the core of *Intensity*. The world-wide plague that wipes out most of humanity in King's *The Stand* is only a few degrees beyond the plagues—diseases, social unrest, political threats—we presently face; his condemnation of abuse in *Dolores Claiborne*, *Insomnia*, and *Rose Madder* most probably strikes home more frequently that we might wish. The fictional disintegration of society in Robert R. McCammon's *Swan Song* or *Mine* or *Stinger* reflects the real disintegrations we see around us. The unique visions these and other similar writers offer of what it is to live here, to live now, is captured in their novels and stories in ways that no alternate form can legitimately duplicate.

And our children read those novels and stories.

Our children see the world in terms of the visions these novels and stories create.

Our children need to understand more completely what it is that these writers are struggling to achieve.

Nor are young readers wholly incapable of understanding the depths of these messages. The Library Discussion Groups gave one evidence to the contrary with their energetic and often surprisingly insightful assessments of King, his works, and his relevance to the students' lives.

And, to be fair about it, so did the teacher's responses to a letter I sent her the day after my son's initial report of what had happened in her class. With perhaps a touch of sarcasm filtering between the lines, I wrote to thank her for mentioning me in her class, and to reassure her that there was indeed sufficient outside resources for her students to exercise their nascent talents for research. In fact, I wrote, if she would be interested, I would be pleased to visit her class and share some of that research with her and her students.

Her response surprised me. No, she did not wish for me to visit her class; instead, she wrote, would I be willing to speak to *all* of the junior English students in two special convocations at the school library during the last two periods of the day, and a third (open to any interested students) after school?

For two hours, I enjoyed talking with the students about what they were reading, why they read King, how his works might relate to their own experiences and lives. In the background, half a dozen English teachers watched as over a hundred students in each session opened up to connect themselves to the words they were reading; and after each session, students and teachers remained behind to discuss what had just happened.

Unfortunately, perhaps, such openness is rare. When one student in Massachusetts—then a freshman at Westfield State College majoring in English—read the original version of this chapter in *The Stephen King Companion*, she wrote me a letter in which she related experiences that paralleled my son's almost exactly. After making the cardinal error of entering her high-school English class the first day with a copy of *The Stand* tucked under her arm ("and my fate was sealed for the year"), she had the temerity to write her term paper on King, using *The Stand*, *Misery*, *The Tommyknockers*, *Skeleton Crew*, *Nightmares & Dreamscapes*, *IT*, and *Four Past Midnight* as primary texts; Tim Underwood, Chuck Miller, and Tony Magistrale provided the secondary materials.

When she handed in the paper, the teacher protested that King was not an acceptable topic. When the class reminded him that he had said that they could write on *anything*, he capitulated. In essence, she had challenged him to evaluate her paper on the basis of her skill at writing rather than on Stephen King's reputation as a writer. "Into the Dark: The Wit and Wisdom of Stephen King" received an honors "A."

The student's final comments were that in college, even if her teachers didn't appreciate King, they at least respected her choice to read him.

Not all students are forced to defend their choices, of course. There are teachers—high school as well as college—who understand that students learn more when they write about authors that are part of their lives. Only a few months after receiving a copy of the first student's essay, I received an E-mail request for help on another high-school term paper. This time there was no hesitance on the teacher's part, and the student was armed with half a dozen possible topics, any one of which could have been developed into a fully realized research paper. We exchanged a few messages (with the Composition Instructor in me suggesting that he focus his thesis, pare down his ambitions, etc.); two months later I received a copy of that essay as well, a carefully written examination of "The Demise of Society as Portrayed by Stephen King," drawing on works by George Beahm, Tony Magistrale, Joseph Reino, Stephen Spignesi, and Douglas E. Winter.

Both of these are, of course, individual examples, perhaps representing extremes of responses to King in the schools, but nevertheless suggesting that academia has not yet decided how to handle such writers. The fact remains that his reputation is as ambivalent among the schoolmasters as it is among the critics. When a student arriving for a conference with a university professor is greeted with a disdainful gesture toward a King novel in a stack of books the student is carrying and a curt "Don't bring trash like that into my office," the dichotomy becomes evident.

VI.

ACORNS TO OAKS: EXPLORATIONS OF THEME, IMAGE, AND CHARACTER IN THE EARLY WORKS OF STEPHEN KING[1]

One of King's most consistent characteristics as a writer is his failure to repeat himself. Each novel, each story he publishes is a self-contained entity that may share themes, settings, even characters from previous novels, but nonetheless moves readers in new and unexpected directions; King does not simply write sequels to bestselling novels to insure another bestseller. While lesser fantasists may be satisfied to repeat time-worn formulae and focus on essentially the same images or use the same literary devices,[2] King manages to bring something new to each new story.

This is not to say, however, that each story stands in strict isolation. Beyond the recurrences noted in other chapters of this study, King also demonstrates a logical and understandable growth from story to story. In fact, many of his early works are memorable less for their own sakes than for the insight they shed on later, more substantive works.

One of his earliest stories, "The Star Invaders," appeared as a self-published chapbook (designed, typed, mimeographed and stapled by King) in 1964. It is an account of human encounters with hostile aliens intent upon taking over the Earth, a dastardly plan foiled only by the strength of character and purpose of the hero, Jed Pierce. In the story, a lesser character, Jerry Hiken, is captured by the aliens, who tortured him to force him to reveal Pierce's secret stronghold. Having withstood the "maximum life-sustaining voltage of the Electroylysis Slab" (4), Hiken is subjected to the ultimate torture—to that which he fears more than anything else:

> Lord, they had locked him in a small room! It seemed even smaller than before. Jerry felt a cold sweat break out on his brow. He remembered back thirty years. He had been a kid then, a really small kid. His father had been a bear on discipline, and ev-

ery time he'd done something wrong, he was locked
in the closet to meditate....
He had gotten to hate that closet. It was small
and stuffed with clothes. The acrid smell of moth-
balls made him cough, and to his terrified four-year-
old mind, it always seemed that a tiger crouched in
the corner. (5)

Now Jerry finds himself locked in a closet again—but a closet with a
vicious twist, It shrinks. Inexorably, almost imperceptibly it grows
smaller until the walls touch him, squeeze him. He screams in anguish
and promises frantically to tell everything; but when the walls retreat,
he again refuses to speak. In the face of this new evidence of human
defiance, the alien says ("implacably," as King specifies in the text):

We can lock you in again....Only this time the
walls will squeeze until the blood runs from your ears
and your nose and even from the little black holes in
the center of your eyes.
It can squeeze you into just a blob of shrieking
protoplasm, if we so desire. (7)

Faced with such terror, Jerry Hiken crumbles and reveals all... then
kills himself by "beat[ing] his head in on the bulkhead of the floor" (8).
By itself, the episode is not particularly noteworthy. The
characterization is flat, the aliens stereotypic, the story itself derivative—nothing unexpected in the writings of a sixteen-year-old story-
teller. But if one looks closely at the episode, especially in light of
King's subsequent productions, something more than the story-as-story
unfolds. Through the clarity of hindsight, the torture-room becomes
recognizable as a prototype of Margaret White's punishment closet in
Carrie, there amplified and developed into a full instrument of horror.
The single reference to tigers in the corner not only captures the naive
terror of a four-year-old for the darkness, but also suggests a more
completely developed narrative line in "Here There Be Tygers," published only four years later in *Ubris*, the University of Maine at Orono
arts magazine. And the final threat of being squeezed to death, the
warning that ultimately unites with his fear of the closet to break Jerry
Hiken's resolve, may in fact be an imagistic kernal for one of King's
most graphic and most effective tales, "The Raft" (1982).

"KING'S GARBAGE TRUCK"

Other examples of King's early exploration of themes and images are readily available. For nearly two years, King contributed
weekly columns to *The Maine Campus*, the college newspaper at UMO.

The columns range from reviews of books and films, to free-wheeling satires, to political and social conscience-raising essays, to forays in autobiography. Many of the columns have a direct bearing on later works. A column on game shows suggests elements of *The Running Man,* for example, while David Bright, mentioned several times as the editor of the paper, would appear as a reporter in *The Dead Zone* and later as a significant character in *The Tommyknockers.* It is fascinating to read the entire sequence of columns in light of later works, but for the purposes of this chapter, two specific examples are enough to show how King's imagination developed.

His first "Garbage Truck" column (20 Feb. 1969) included a review of a program called *Why We Dance* presented at Goddard College. The production was bad and good, he notes, but

> ...the good was very good, the best being a terrifying piece called *Child of Our Darkness*...featuring Wynde Winston.... Miss Winston, portraying a child-woman torn between forces of light and darkness, was very good indeed. The conclusion, with burning flames projected onto her body and a screen behind her, was almost numbing in impact—a Joan of Arc for our times, perhaps. (9)

It takes little imagination to develop this description into an imagistic compression of the character that would become Carrie White... or perhaps even Charlie McGee. Later in the same column, King describes Bette Davis in *Hush...Hush, Sweet Charlotte* as a "malevolent Shirley Temple in her bangs and puffy-armed white dresses," who "crawls slowly down that shadowy, decayed stairway letting out the most godawful sounds you have ever heard. Mary Poppins she ain't, but then, I have a feeling she could eat Julie Andrews for dinner with Dick Van Dyke for dessert" (9). Here we find, in embryonic as well as archetypal form, the "monstrous woman" that figures in one of King's earliest short stories, "The Blue Air Compressor" (1971), and recurs almost without exception throughout his subsequent novels, culminating (to date at least) in Annie Wilkes, Paul Sheldon's "number one fan" in *Misery.*

In a second—and in some ways most intriguing—example from the "Garbage Truck" essays, King transcribed a letter he had written on 26 February 1969 as the March 19th column. The letter described the "Big Snowstorm of '69" and its physical and psychological effects on King. "I think I must be writing you because of the snow," he begins:

104

All this snow. It sets off strange thoughts in the head—or at least in my head, which is always filled with middling strange thoughts....

Almost wish it would keep on forever and bury everything, the stupid passions, pointless lusts, the pollution, the pretentious ideas, the crap and the crud—the skiers and the swimmers, the tobogganers and the campers alike....

The power fails—the emergency generators are gone. The record on the jukebox dies—guitars, drums, and organ elongating, deepening, dying. Snow, fine as sand, whirlpools under the doors. And these last [people] sit at their tables in the cool blue darkness of February....Their fingers grow numb, and toes—frost on the silverware in delicate lacework patterns. Coffee sludge freezes in the bottoms of cups. A darkness that fell early. Breath in frosty plumes. A final, frozen silence. No more fire, ice this time.

Morbid, but oddly beautiful. Big world out there, big dark, little us. Very little. All of us inscribed in our magic circles, hidden under eyeshadow and beards, under beads and buttons like cave-people cowering under rocks. We play with reality with all the confidence of a baby playing with a pistol. We give it names. We cling to each other.(5)3

Eleven years later, that sequence of images and ideas reappears in fictive form, as Stella Flanders affirms in "Do the Dead Sing" that

the Reach was wider in those days and when the wind roared and the surf pounded and the dark came early, why, we felt very small—no more than dust motes in the mind of God. So it was natural for us to join hands, one with the other.

We joined hands, children, and if there were times when we looked too long at the summer's flowers, it was only because we had heard the wind and the waters on long winter nights, and we were afraid.4

As Stella rejoins her dead husband Bill, and then meets Madelaine Stoddard, and Annabelle Frane and the other dead, King reinforces the image of a humanity huddling together in a circle of warmth and light as their only protection against the darkness—only now, there is less to fear and more to wonder at:

> They stood in a circle in the storm, the dead of
> Goat Island, and the wind screamed around them,
> driving its packet of snow, and some kind of song
> burst from her. It went up into the wind and the wind
> carried it away. They all sang then, as children will
> sing in their high, sweet voices as a summer evening
> draws down to summer night. They sang, and Stella
> felt herself going to them and with them, finally
> across the Reach. There was a bit of pain, but not
> much; losing her maidenhead had been worse. They
> stood in a circle in the night. The snow blew around
> them and they sang. They sang, and—5

With that passage, a letter written in response to a snowstorm completes its transformation into a powerful story about death and change, about humanity and fear, that itself is capable of transforming its readers.

"SLADE"

In a substantially lighter vein, King followed his "Garbage Truck" columns with an eight-installment parody of Western fiction called "Slade" (June-August 1970). Essentially a *jeu-d'esprit*—perhaps reflecting his recent graduation from UMO—the story reverberates with off-the-wall humor, with puns, with conscious inversions of every conceivable convention of the Western and equally conscious repetitions of every conceivable cliché—verbal, situational, and characterizational. At a moment of crisis in Chapter 7 (30 July 1970), Slade confronts the villains, Sam Columbine, owner of the Rotten Vulture ranch, and his "A-No.-1 Top Gun, Pinky Lee"—King notes that the "only two men in the American Southwest that could even approach 'Pinky' for pure, dad-ratted evil were Hunchback Fred Agnew (who Slade gunned down three weeks ago) and Sam Columbine himself" (6). Now, at the showdown, Pinky Lee

> dropped to his chest, fanning the hammer of his sin-
> ister Buntline Special. Slade felt bullets race all
> around him. He fired back twice, but—curse!—the
> hammers of his two sinister .45's only clicked on
> empty chambers. He had forgotten to load up after
> downing the three badmen back at the Rotten Vulture.
> Lee rolled to cover behind a barrel of taco chips.
> Columbine was already crouched behind a giant bottle
> of mayonnaise that had been air-dropped a month be-
> fore after the worst flood disaster in American South-
> west history (why drop mayonnaise after a flood dis-
> aster? none of your damn business). (6)

Taco Chips? Mayonnaise? Hunchback Fred Agnew? (Any relation to a certain vice-president?)

In a *Western?*

But King carries it off. There is such energy, such a sense of fun (even in the non-chapter that details attempts by UMO administrators to censor the story) that it all works, demonstrating that the "King of Horror" also possesses a strong (if occasionally warped) sense of humor.

Yet what is even more intriguing—and more relevant in terms of his later stories—is his attitude toward Slade. The opening paragraph of chapter 1 (11 June 1970) hints at the satire and parody to follow, but at the same time, it introduces an intriguing figure:

> It was almost dark when Slade rode into Dead Steer Springs. He was tall in the saddle, a grim-faced man dressed all in black. Even the handles of his two sinister .45's, which rode low on his hips were black. Ever since the early 1870's, when the name of Slade had begun to strike fear into the stoutest of Western hearts, there had been many whispered legends about his dress. One story had it that he wore black as a perpetual emblem of mourning for his Illinois sweetheart, Miss Polly Peachtree of Paduka, who passed tragically from this vale of tears when a flaming Montgolfier balloon crashed into the Peachtree barn while Polly was milking the cows. But some said he wore black because Slade was the Grim Reaper's agent in the American Southwest—the devil's hangman. And then there were some who thought he was queerer than a three-dollar bill. No one, however, advanced this last idea to his face. (4).

Discounting for the moment the obvious comic elements, the consciously over-blown genre rhetoric, and the slighting reference to homosexuality (another recurrent motif throughout King's works), what remains evokes the dark man, the man in black, the archetypal gunfighter, the mysterious wanderer of the Western wastes—in a word, the central figure of *The Dark Tower* novels. In the series of stories originally published in *The Magazine of Fantasy & Science Fiction* from October 1978 through November 1981, reprinted in *The Dark Tower: The Gunslinger*, and continued in *The Dark Tower: The Drawing of the Three*, and *The Dark Tower: The Waste Lands*, King adroitly transforms the comic Slade into the epic-tragic Dark Man, Roland, and initiates the tale of the quest for the Dark Tower. The first lines of "The Gunslinger," the earliest published chapter of the Dark Tower quest, echo the opening atmosphere of "Slade": "The man in black fled across the desert, and the gunslinger followed." A few paragraphs later, we read:

> Below the waterbag were his guns, finely weighted to his hand. The two belts crisscrossed above his crotch. The holsters were oiled too deeply for even this Philistine sun to crack. The stocks of the guns were sandalwood, yellow and finely grained. The holsters were tied down with rawhide cord, and they swung heavily against his hips. The brass casings of the cartridges looped into the gunbelts twinkled and flashed and heliographed in the sun. The leather made subtle creaking noises. The guns themselves made no noise. They had spilled blood. There was no need to make noise in the sterility of the desert.[6]

Shorn of all comic pretenses, here is the essence of Slade: Roland, the gunslinger, initiating one of King's most ambitious narratives to date.

THE POETRY

Given what was happening in "Slade," published in mid-1970, it is not surprising that one of King's first published poems, published in 1969, was "The Dark Man." The immediate imagistic connection between a comic-Western "dark man" and the poem suggests not only King's immediate interest in that particular figure, but more generally the relationship between King's poetry (almost all published between 1968 and 1971) and his larger body of fiction. As with the other early works discussed so far, their interest lies less in their inherent value as poems than in their value as indices to King's mind and development. Although the poems often demonstrate what his detractors might consider unusual perceptivity and sensitivity for the "King of Horror," they do not rivet the reader's attention to the same extent as his stories and novels. One reason for that is simply that King excels in longer forms. In spite of his objection that critics and reviewers automatically discount the literary value of longer novels, he is pragmatically aware that his readers do not. His longest works—especially *The Stand* (both versions) and *IT*—are among his best, his most popular, and his most durable. Certainly the promise of an unexpurgated *The Stand*, restoring substantial portions of the original manuscript, stirred great interest among his readership, with few arguing that the novel was already too long; reader response to the "Complete & Uncut Edition" was immediate and powerfully positive. His published statements that *The Dark Tower: The Gunslinger* and *The Dark Tower: The Drawing of the Three* were only the opening episodes in a quest-narrative that could easily exceed 3,000 pages when completed have done little to turn away read-ers—public pressure to read the novel was so great that he was finally forced to reverse an earlier decision not to release them for mass production *because* they were long, incomplete, and unlike anything else he had yet written. As these works clearly indicate, one of King's strengths is his ability to orchestrate huge movements, to weave his fine threads into an enormous tapestry that rivets interest on the larger as well as on the smaller elements.

By virtue of their form, however, his poems work against that approach. They focus on the small, on the minute. They are not them-selves trivial, but they communicate implicitly a sense of triviality when set next to the vastly ambitious bulk of *The Stand, IT,* or *Insomnia,* for example, or even the lesser bulk of *Carrie, 'Salem's Lot, Dolores Clai-borne,* and the other novels. Yet, as with the "The Star Invaders," "Garbage Truck" columns, and "Slade," the poems—especially the ear-liest of them—are fascinating in the light they shed on King's interests and imagination. In fact, the earliest poem, when viewed again under the clear light of superior hindsight, becomes virtually a catalog of themes and techniques that would soon become increasingly important.

By 1968, King had already professionally published four sto-ries and completed the manuscript for *The Long Walk* (published essen-tially unrevised in 1979). In the fall of that year, "Harrison State Park '68" appeared in *Ubris,* a UMO publication. It is a relatively long, el-liptical poem of 100 free verse lines, with stanzas spaced erratically across its two pages. It is, at first glance, experimental and ex-ploratory, as befits the time and circumstances of its composition—the work of a twenty-year-old, socially and politically active college stu-dent in the late sixties. The subject is a murder in nearby Harrison State Park, a location mentioned in several later novels. As a poem, it is not particularly strong. It relies on verbal clichés ("If you can't be an athlete,/be an athletic supporter"), overt puns ("call me Ishmael/i am a semen") that sometimes form only tangential connections with the rest of the poem, and elliptical images so compressed as to be virtually un-approachable. And even at the time it was written, the use of frag-mented white space to create poetic texture had become a visual cliché. In addition, the text shifts from full use of capitals to erratic use of lower case *i* for the first-person pronoun, while equally erratic punctua-tional devices ("can't" with the apostrophe in one stanza, "dont" with-out it in another) occasionally impede the movement of the poem.

However, in spite of those difficulties (not surprising in the work of a youthful poet), "Harrison State Park '68" repays reading. It begins with what would become a trademark in King's fictions: head-note quotations to suggest the focus of the story to follow. In this case—as with *IT,* which pairs a quotation from William Carlos Williams's *Patterson* with a line from Bruce Springsteen—the passages are carefully juxtaposed to create a sense of internal tension: Thomas

Szasz's "All mental disorders are simply defective strategies for handling difficult life situations" collides in context, vocabulary, structure, and meaning with Ed Sanders's "And I feel like homemade shit."

Yet the headnotes are effective and appropriate. The poem deals with tension, with conflict, with juxtaposition of images. The feeling created by the lines "*Modern Screen Romances* is a tent on the grass/Over a dozen condoms/in a quiet box," with its quiescent evocation of sexuality and illusion, clashes with the poem's horrific conclusion:

> oh
> dont
> please touch me
> but dont
> dont
> and i reach for your hand
> but touch only the radiating five pencils
> of your bones:
> —Can you do it?

Throughout the poem there are additional elements that will become standard in the vintage King. The repetition of "—Can you do it?" suggests the incremental "Do you love" of "The Raft" and "Do the Dead Sing?"/"The Reach". The stanzas include multiple brandname references—Sony, Westinghouse, Playtex living bras, Fig Newtons—and cultural icons such as the Doors and Sonny and Cher. But, as is appropriate in a work of this length, each of these themes and techniques remains rudimentary, suggested more than completed.

More powerful as an independent work, and more indicative of the directions King's imagination would take, however, is "The Dark Man," published in the Spring 1969 of *Ubris* and the 1970 issue of *Moth* (also a UMO publication, with Burton Hatlen as advisor). The differences between "Harrison State Park '68" and "The Dark Man" are striking. The earlier poem seems verbally and visually diffuse. It lacks a clear focus for its elliptical and imagistic approach to violence. The later poem, on the other hand, begins with strong, almost stridently violent imagery, and supports that strength throughout:

> i have stridden the fuming way
> of sun-hammered tracks and
> smashed cinders....

Subsequent stanzas repeat the opening syntactical structure, "i have...i have...i have," creating a powerful rhythm that carries throughout the poem. Images are both implicitly and explicitly violent, rough, horrific, and include "desperate houses with counterfeit chimneys," "glaring swamps/where musk-reek rose/to mix with the sex smell of rotting cypress stumps...," and

> i forced a girl in a field of wheat
> and left her sprawled with the virgin bread
> a savage sacrifice.

The poem concludes simply and abruptly with a devastating assertion of identity: "i am a dark man."

To King's readers, of course, the phrase "dark man" resonates with meaning. The Dark Man is nearly as consistent a motif in King's works as the Monstrous Woman. One dark man, Roland, is the key figure in the Dark Tower cycle, while another, Randall Flagg, is at the center of *The Stand* and *The Eyes of the Dragon* (and peripherally in *The Dark Tower* novels as well). King's initial description of Flagg in *The Stand* echoes the general atmosphere and feeling, and at times even the specific metrical rhythms and vocabulary, of the poem. In the five pages of Chapter 17 in the original version (Chapter 23 in the 1990 edition), paragraphs incessantly repeat similar syntactical openings: "Randall Flagg, the dark man, strode south..."; "He walked rapidly...," "He walked south...," "He moved on...," "He moved on...," "He *hammered* along...," "He rocked along...," "The dark man walked and smiled," "He strode on...," and "He stopped" [my italics]. Only in the final three paragraphs does King shift to another structural form—and the shift is significant because Flagg suddenly becomes aware that "His time of transfiguration was at hand. He was going to be born for the second time...."[7] Like the speaker of the final line of the poem, Randall Flagg becomes simply the Dark Man.

In addition, the images in *The Stand* parallel those sketched in the poem. In a sequence that echoes the rape imagery of the final stanza of the poem, King writes of Flagg that

> The women he took to bed with him, even if they had
> reduced intercourse to something as casual as getting a
> snack from the refrigerator, accepted him with a stiff-
> ening of the body, a turning away of the countenance.
> Sometimes they accepted him with tears. They took
> him the way they might take a ram with golden eyes
> or a black dog—and when it was done they were *cold*,
> so *cold*, it seemed impossible they could ever be warm
> again.[8]

As does the speaker of the poem, Flagg exists in a world embued with violence and terror:

He hammered along, arms swinging by his sides. He was known, well known, along the highways in hiding that are traveled by the poor and the mad, by the professional revolutionaries and by those who have been taught to hate so well that their hate shows on their faces like harelips and they are unwelcome except by others like them, who welcome them to cheap rooms with slogans and posters on the walls, to basements where lengths of sawed-off pipe are held in padded vises while they are stuffed with high explosives, to back rooms where lunatic plans are laid: to kill a cabinet member, to kidnap the child of a visiting dignitary, or to break into a boardroom meeting of Standard Oil with grenades and machines guns and murder in the name of the people.[9]

In the rhythms, alliterations, and periods of that final extended sentence, even in passages that can be scanned as iambic/dactylic meter, one can hear echoes of similar lines in "The Dark Man." The poem is only forty-two-lines long, divided into five stanzas. Yet the images and meanings the poem suggests have required the major portions of five novels to explore more fully.

The other two King poems published in *Moth* have less impact, perhaps they are narrower in focus. "Silence" is a twelve-line monologue, superficially suggestive of King's later poem "Paranoid: A Chant" in its obsession with "the feary silence of fury." "Donovan's Brain" is, as the title indicates, a reflection on the fifties horror-film by that title, again an exercise in obsession and terror—the latter signalled by typographical placement in the center of the page and bracketed by asterisks:

****

horror

****

Its combination of filmic echoes and strident imagery—"warped and sucked by desert wine/raped by the brain of that monstrous man"—moves King a step closer to devices that will press insistently against the texture of his fictions.

A year later, an untitled poem appeared in the January 1971 issue of *Onan*. There is less here to consider, in part because of the subject: fishing. At a time when King was writing not only tales of horror and terror for *Cavalier* and *Startling Mystery Stories* but also generally mainstream novels—*Rage, The Long Walk, Sword in the Darkness* (an unpublished race-riot novel), and *Blaze* (an unpublished reworking of Steinbeck's *Of Mice and Men*)—is should not surprise that his poetic imagination might turn to mainstream images as well. The poem is twenty-four-lines long, a meditation on sport and responsibility that concludes with the discovery that when the first is overwhelmed by the second, it is time to "put away our poles." Still, even here, there is an increasing sense of control in the lines. The images are less violent, less vigorous, but more disciplined.

King's increasing maturity is also evident in his next published poem, a paean to baseball called "Brooklyn August" (*Io*, 1971). Again, the subject militates against any substantive influence on King's major novels, except to the extent that baseball touches on the lives of characters, as in épisodes of *IT* and elsewhere. Of some interest, however, is the overt structure of the poem, a blend of traditional poetry and the rhythms of prose. Three rhyming sequences of lines (all with terminal long-*o* rhymes) are intercut with free-verse descriptive stanzas that move baseball from an idealized national pastime to a sometimes dark reality. The return to rhyming couplets reminiscent of Eliot's famous:

> In the room the women come and go
> Talking of Michelangelo

from "The Love Song of J. Alfred Prufrock" (even using the same terminal rhyme sound) suggests a dissociation of perception as the poem shifts from repetitive, formal statements couched in rhyming couplets to the minutiae of observation expressed through free verse and the rhythms of prose. The poet's vision is expanding, incorporating not only his own observations but also tags of literary heritage as well (as in the reference to Poe in "The Glass Floor" [1967] and "The Blue Air Compressor" [1971]). In later works, such allusions would become increasingly complex and important, from the multiple literary references in *The Shining*, to the assertion of an essentially Lovecraftian universe in *IT*, to the references in to King's fictive world in *The Tommyknockers*. King's arsenal of allusions would eventually incorporate Melville, Lovecraft, Yeats, Frost, Hemingway, Faulkner, Milton, Orwell, Tolkien, Wells, Stoker, Dickens, Shakespeare, Golding, Coleridge, O'Casey, and literally dozens of others—a tempering of classical and traditional literary elements to balance even more numerous contemporary and pop-culture references to Bob Dylan, The Who, John Jakes, Bruce Springsteen, and the like. "Brooklyn August" lies a long way from the focus of King's major works, but even there—and even this early—one of his fundamental structural devices is clearly demonstrated.

What can one say in summary following this brief excursion through some of King's less accessible early works.

That the child is, as Wordsworth says, the father of the man?

Yes, certainly.

That an author's early interests may find place in his later, more mature works?

Again, certainly yes.

That writers are often derivative when they begin and only gradually develop a significant personal voice?

Yes, again.

But beyond that, this survey suggests something more direct about King. His reputation is obvious. He is the "King of Horror." He freely indulges in graphic sexuality and violence; in socially unacceptable language; in images that horrify, terrify, or—failing that—simply *gross out*. Academicians frequently disparage him. High school teachers often ignore him. Concerned parents of teen-aged readers sometimes abhor him.

But these surface elements in his writings and his reputation sometimes obscure a deeper understanding—that he is not essentially a *horror* writer. *Salem's Lot* is about vampires; *The Shining* has a haunted hotel—and haunted parents; "The Raft" has a monster; *IT* incorporates an almost encyclopedic exploration of monsters, fear, and terror. But other novels and stories deny such easy classification. *The Dead Zone* is not a horror novel, although horrible things happen. *Carrie, Cujo, Firestarter, Misery, The Tommyknockers, Dolores Claiborne, Insomnia, The Green Mile* (to date, at least)—these are less horror than stories of psychological suspense punctuated to varying degrees with overtones of science fiction or dark fantasy.

In his finest, most focused works—stories such as "The Reach," for example—King attains a transcendence that clearly elevates him beyond the simplistic genre classification of a "horror writer." And many of the images, themes, even characters that appear in his strongest works have a clear ancestry stretching back to his first imaginings. What he wrote in "The Star Invaders" or the "Garbage Truck" columns or "Slade" or the early poetry may not have been intrinsically important; what those works provided in giving play to his rapidly developing vision, however, was.

Acorns to oaks....

Small beginnings to vast, panoramic works that have changed an entire industry, that have guided the imaginations of a generation of readers and writers, that have defined concisely and perhaps definitively three decades of American society, and that have altered our perceptions of literature, of our culture, our times, and our world.

VII.

BEGINNINGS:
"KING'S GARBAGE TRUCK"

During his last two years at the University of Maine in Orono, King developed rapidly as a writer. He had already completed many projects, including publishing "I Was a Teenage Grave Robber," "The Glass Floor," "Cain Rose Up," "Here There Be Tygers," the original version of "Strawberry Spring," "The Reaper's Image," "Night Surf," and "Stud City"; he had begun what would finally appear as the first Bachman novel, *Rage*, as well as manuscripts for *The Long Walk* and an unpublished novel, *Sword in the Darkness*.

Even more importantly, in terms of working with a reading public, he wrote columns for *The Maine Campus*, the weekly college newspaper; his wife Tabitha notes that he had become a "campus institution" even then.[1] From February, 1969 through May, 1970, King published articles discussing topics from the space program to campus politics, from reviews of the season's offerings on television to meditations on change, isolation, and death. Many of the pieces show little that is distinctively Stephen King; others could have come from no other imagination. But all suggest the multiple ways King developed his unique voice as well as indicating underlying experiential sources for key images in several of his later novels and stories. The columns provide insight into King's interests, then and now, and occasionally lead to new understandings of characters and situations in novels published a decade or two later. And, on a larger scale, they are themselves entries in a cultural history of sorts, since the subjects King chose to explore are often those most important to his audience, the college students of the late 1960s and early 1970s—many of whom now make up a large portion of his reading public.

The "Garbage Truck" columns have not been reprinted; the originals are available only at the UMO archives. Since they often suggest intriguing avenues of thought, however, it is worthwhile to indicate what the columns cover. The following summaries give the date, pagination, and approximate word count for each, along with indications of how some might have influenced King's subsequent writings.

20 February 1969: 9 (642 words): King's first column reviews the Goddard College Dancers and the film *Hush...Hush, Sweet Charlotte*. In the former, King was particularly impressed with Wynde Winston and John Caldwell's *Child of Our Darkness*, which concluded with special lighting effects projecting flames onto Winston and a screen behind her in an image "almost numbing in impact—a Joan of Arc for our times, perhaps." It may also, perhaps, have provided a kernel image for *Firestarter*. The film is impressive, King continues, for Bette Davis's performance as a "malevolent Shirley Temple in her bangs and puffy-armed white dresses," a foretaste of the "monstrous women" King developed in his fiction as early as "The Blue Air Compressor" (1971). King recommends the film for fans of frightening films and of Bette Davis.

27 February 1969: 7 (515 words): The second column reviews Franco Zeffirelli's *Romeo and Juliet*. King notes that Shakespeare is usually treated "in the same way porcupines make love—very cautiously"; as a result students are intimidated by his reputation and by his language. In Zeffirelli's hands, however, the old tale receives new life, augmented by strong performances by Olivia Hussey ("merely perfect") and Leonard Whiting. The result is a production of Shakespeare as different from most as Kool-Aid differs from straight Jack Daniels.

6 March 1969: 9 (515 words): In the "RICHARD BACHMAN" novel *The Running Man*, the true villain is the Network. Society suffers at the mercy of media manipulated by greedy and unscrupulous men. This column reads almost like an early sketch of ideas for *The Running Man* as King describes the game shows he thinks the television networks should offer: *The Middle-Aged Game*, with Bud Collyer, in which contestants try to tie their shoelaces and identify cigarettes containing hallucinogenic drugs; *The Brutality Game*, with Dick Daley and a battle between forty Chicago policemen and a studio audience composed of hippies, pacifists, minorities, and college professors (a game suggesting one scene restored in "The Complete & Uncut Edition of *The Stand*);[2] *The Divorce Game*, with Zsa Zsa Gabor, with an audience-judged discussion among three divorcing couples; *The Wife-Swapping Game*, with Dr. Joyce Brothers; and *The Burial Game*, with Vincent Price and teams composed of two members—one living and the other dead (this one suggesting a central theme in *Dolores Claiborne*). Given these possibilities, King argues, the networks themselves could surely come up with something more innovative than *The Newlywed Game*.

13 March 1969: 7 (690 words): In a satirical vein, King reveals a plot at UMO to do away with mediocrity; readers can stand up for mediocrity, he urges, by attending the Bangor Cinema and watching *Born Wild*, then playing the latest Tammy Wynette album, *Stand by Your*

116

Man. The next step is to go to Mr. Paperback and buy William Goldman's *Boys and Girls Together*—and in doing so make National Mediocrity Week successful.

20 March 1969: 7 (670 words): In an attempt at creating a writer-audience dialogue, King asks his readers to tell him what they remember—the important memories that changed their lives in critical ways. King's list includes seeing Elvis Presley at the community Theater, listening to Jerry Lee Lewis and Little Richard, and playing Rock-Breaks-Scissors; he also reminisces about his first kiss by a "not-aunt-or-mother female," Davey Crockett hats, and hula-hoops. The piece is curiously nostalgic, as if King were already aware of the 1960s as a watershed in American cultural history; in a number of his novels, characters' reminiscences of key moments in the 1960s—music, films, cultural icons of varying sorts—surface at critical moments.

29 March 1969: 7 (600 words): King presents several responses to his "Do You Remember" column, including such specifics as 1950s clothing; the Lone Ranger and Tonto; radio horror programs that kids weren't supposed to listen to, such as *Inner Sanctum* and *I Love a Mystery* ; and Republic serials at the theater. He concludes that "Somehow everything seems to get just a little dirtier and more selfish as we get older. It's good to remember other times, once in a while," a statement that could stand as epigram for *IT*.

10 April 1969: 6 (580 words): In another dual column, King reviews *The Lion in Winter* and William Castle's *The Riot*. Of the former he says that "the dialogue is lusciously biting and the acting is poisonously perfect," particularly in performances by Peter O'Toole and Katharine Hepburn, but it is not as satisfying as Zeffirelli's *Romeo and Juliet*. *The Riot*, loosely based on Frank Elli's novel, is a "gay carnival of violence, homosexuality, and imbecility," far less impressive than Paul Muni's film, *I Am a Fugitive from a Chain Gang*.

17 April 1969: 7, 13 (740 words): As part of a United Artists publicity campaign, King and representatives of about forty other college newspapers were invited to New York to preview *Popi* and *If It's Tuesday, This Must Be Belgium*. King found both films mildly interesting, almost successful in what they attempted. Of more lasting importance, however, were his impressions of the plasticity and superficiality of New York: "You can get seven TV channels, but the air smells bad." It may be significant that few of his later works use New York—or any large cities—as major settings; certainly his descriptions of the city in *The Stand* reflect his comments here.

24 April 1969: 11 (690 words): King introduces himself as President Emeritus of the N.G.U.T.S.C.M.C. (the "Nitty Gritty Up Tight Society for a Campus With More Cools," pronounced "nuhguts-mick"), and as such calls for a general student strike unless several demands are met: courses in black literature and black history, as well as other courses for minorities and special interests, including Plumbing 1 and 2, The Art of Mandarin Fingernail Growing, etc.; birth control vending machines in every dorm (in the interest of female liberation, of course); elimination of curfew; removal of the bookstore, and its replacement by an "educational discotheque"; and the abolition of the university itself as a cause of pollution, inflation, and other diseases. Without a university, of course, there could be no student strikes, and thus the entire problem could be resolved.

1 May 1969: 7 (600 words): During the Fall semester of 1968, King participated in an experimental seminar in Contemporary Poetry under the leadership of Burton Hatlen and Jim Bishop. King is excited by the chance to read poetry by "writers who aren't dust yet," including Ron Loewinsohn who, King notes, will be reading at the University in four days. The column also mentions the recent UMO poetry festival, in which Howard Nemerov, Constance Hunting, and Richard Wilbur participated. Unfortunately, King finds the latter already too strongly entrenched as part of the literary establishment—Loewinsohn is not: he is "a gut-writer, a belly-writer." The column indicates King's interest in poetry, as well as defining a number of his early critical criteria.

8 May 1969: 6 (914 words): The column begins with a question: "Want me to tell you a bad thing?" and from there anatomizes the fears and frustrations King and others felt as college students in the late sixties, epitomized by the simple act of waking in the middle of the night and wondering what you are doing. The column is strengthened by King's use of individuals to symbolize the malaise of his generation: a girl suddenly bursting into tears in the middle of dinner; Sally Socialite, unprepared for the life she will lead in suburban American (a hint at *Gerald's Game* and *Rose Madder*); Harry Harried, highly strung and about to enter a job market that will give him his first heart-attack by age thirty-seven (this paragraph reads almost like a character study for Billy Halleck in *Thinner*). It defines the pressure cooker of life in a university where the last syllabus "looked just a little too standardized, a little too much like a cheap cop-out." The result: perhaps a too-real daydream about climbing a tower with a rifle and picking off a few students (cf. "Cain Rose Up," first published 1968; "Apt Pupil" in *Different Seasons*), or just listening to Bob Dylan's *Ballad of a Thin Man*.

15 May 1969: 7 (715 words): The piece is divided into four segments, each bracketed by the repeated word *ugly*. The first, in present-tense, places King in an "End the War" rally, along with Chris Harstedt, Judy Bowie, David Bright (cf. the reporter in *The Dead Zone*, chapter 9, and the last quarter of *The Tommyknockers*), Dick Lindsay, and Larry Moscowitz. The march is highlighted by violence: someone throws an egg at them; Harstedt is shoved away from the banner; King is hit in the stomach. In the second part, they are pelted by eggs and rocks; one girl is stunned that people would throw things at her. Part Three details a confrontation with a fraternity group: "I don't know what is said. All I see are fraternity sweatshirts. Behind them I see Gestapo figures burning books and Jews." There is the threat of real violence that never materializes. Part Four shifts to an impromptu speech by an Army Veteran on the importance of winning the war in Vietnam; Bright speaks about the immorality of fighting in a war he can't believe in. The piece ends with King leaving the rally and hearing a snatch of "The Ballad of the Green Berets" that crystalizes the moment in the same way that rock lyrics crystalize crucial moments for characters in his subsequent novels and stories.

22 May 1969: 7 (780 words): King reacts to a nominee for the University Board of Trustees, concerned by what he sees as double-dealing during a meeting of the Coalition for Peace in Viet Nam, of which King and the nominee were both members. When a vote went against the nominee, he threatened to withdraw from the Coalition unless a second vote were taken. When a re-vote also went against him, the nominee again threatened to leave the Coalition. A third vote went in his favor. King is less concerned about the specific issue than about the undercutting of the democratic process involved. Looking toward immediate and serious problems—an impending clash over ROTC on campus, a possible incursion of the SDS (Students for a Democratic Society)—King expresses his concern that the nominee would be unable to handle such crises responsibly.

12 June 1969: 4 (518 words): After several serious columns, King lets go with "Boom! and all at once it's summer." The article celebrates summer: lilacs, and sexy films at the drive-ins, and girls walking around in summer dresses. King promises not to get too serious—and gives an overview of some possible columns for the summer *Campus*, including reviews of *Doctor Zhivago* and *The Green Slime*; a review of the Johnny Cash show; an article on pop music. In the meantime, he advises, relax, go to the coast (he mentions Bar Harbor, prominent in *Thinner*) or just sit back and enjoy a cold beer. "Boom! It's great."

20 June 1969: 6 (528 words): In mock-"Dear Abby" style, King becomes "Dear Stevie" and answers such critical questions as whether French kissing can cause pregnancy, whether it is humane to put a mother-in-law with a broken leg out of her misery, whether it is wrong to indulge in unnatural sex practices ("Not if you know enough unnatural girls"), what to do if one's Peace Corps son sends home a shrunken head from Haiti, and, finally, whether King ever gets tired of the "disgusting tripe you turn out in the *Campus*," the latter question from the staff at the *Bangor Daily News*.

27 June 1969: 5, 6 (878 words): King reviews paperbacks available at Bangor's Mr. Paperback, including Robert Bloch's *The Dead Beat*, with its "jolly graveyard humor" counterpointed with terror; Richard Matheson's *The Shrinking Man*, which King considers a tour-de-force; Michael Avallone's *The Coffin Things*, a diatribe against smoking that evolves into "as poisonous a piece of black humor as ever has come your way" (cf. "Quitters, Inc."); and Bram Stoker's *Dracula*, still the classic horror novel and, parenthetically, the novel against which King's own *'Salem's Lot*, his second novel, is most frequently measured.

4 July 1969: 4 (790 words): In assessing the Beatles' impact on rock music, pop music, and contemporary culture, King says that "They have revolutionized hair styles, yanked the average girl's hemline up a foot since 1957, become a moving part in the new drug culture, and have even been part of the wedge that has been breaking ground for a new morality that would have seemed science-fictiony ten years ago." More recently, the group has been instrumental in returning the "beat" to rock and roll—which leads King into a brief review of *The Ballad of John and Yoko*, concentrating on its merging of energy and discipline.

11 July 1969: 5 (1000 words): As he looks forward to Neil Armstrong's first moon walk, King explores his own reactions to the advances being made in space—and discovers two contradictory responses, divided between his conscious self and "the guy in the attic" of his mind. The column details a dream ("I suspect someone of a religious mind might call it a vision") in which a routine transmission from Apollo 11 becomes enmeshed in terror: "A huge, timeless wind has swept down on them and their puny ship, a cyclopean gale from no place that is sweeping them off their neatly computerized orbit and into the gaping germless maw of deep space itself." What remains, after the dream has passed, is the hope that once man finally takes that first step on an alien world, "there is nothing waiting for us in the dark." In its own way, the column indicates King's ambivalence toward science fiction itself, his tendency in ostensibly SF stories such as "The Jaunt," "Beachworld," *Firestarter*, and *The Tommyknockers*, to transform the paraphernalia of science and of science fiction into horror and thrust his readers into the darkness that awaits.

18 July 1969: 7 (880 words): The NGUTSCMC announces its awards for outstanding film performances, including Best Actor (Donald O'Connor, for "playing second banana to an ass for nine years" in the Francis films and still coming out "smelling like a rose"); Best Lousy Movie (*The Good, the Bad, and the Ugly*); Most Nauseating Actress (Elizabeth Taylor); Most Nauseating Actor (Michael J. Pollard); and— more seriously—a list of the ten best films of the past twenty-five years: *Romeo and Juliet, Point Blank, The Hustler, Psycho, The Last Mile, Picnic, Rebel Without a Cause, High Noon, Mildred Pierce*, with number ten left up to the reader to choose. In style and content, the column suggests King's later "Lists That Matter."

25 July 1969: 5, 6 (950 words): As a "tired old hack of 21-going-on-seventy," King sits back and watches the new batch of UMO freshmen as they struggle to adapt, reminiscing about his own experiences as a freshman. The naiveté and trust in freshmen makes him feel like he's "been through the mill."

1 August 1969: 4, 7 (790 words): King tackles the question of birth control, arguing that of all the people on earth, the one he would least like to be would be the pope, not the least because of his unpopular stand on birth control. Yet ultimately King agrees with the pope, although not for the expected reasons. King takes a stand against the pill, opting instead for Norman Mailer's suggestion of legalized abortion. Only then would the moral grounds be clearly defined: abortion is murder, which the individual may or may not consider justifiable. Birth control distances the individual from the consequences of his or her action; the specter of abortion forces clear-cut choices. "So if the population must be controlled, it seems to me that legal murder—abortion—is the only really moral way it can be done. If nothing else, it would force the person involved to come to a serious decision about birth control—and death control."

8 August 1969: 4 (930 words): The column lists a number of UMO people King considers particularly important in his life, including Robert Hunting, Carroll F. Terrell, James Bishop, and Burton Hatlen of the UMO English department; Dave Bright, a fellow staff-worker on *The Daily Campus* who appears briefly in *The Dead Zone* and at greater length in *The Tommyknockers* as a strongly sympathetic newspaper reporter; and others who introduced him to new areas of music, literature, and life.

18 September 1969: 7 (780 words): In an introduction to the new school year, King releases a number of frustrations felt by many (if not most) college students—whom he addresses with a jaunty "Hello, suckers." In spite of the most common reasons for attending the university—family pressures as parents ensure that their offspring will get everything they did not, and the pressures of friends to attend—few students will in fact leave with a true education. In the process of completing the four years, students will face frustrations, red tape, emotional and psychological pressures (cf. "Cain Rose Up"), idiotic requirements and equally idiotic required courses, drugs—and the prospect of suicide...two for "every 15,000 students now tripping the light fantastic on college campuses."

25 September 1969: 5 (790 words): A repeat of the 1 August 1969 column on birth control.

3 October 1969: 5 (550 words): King argues against certain social groups on the UMO campus, particularly the "administration-oriented groups" that seem not to have changed with the times.

9 October 1969: 5 (750 words): In an extensive review of Peter Fonda's *Easy Rider*, King points to the film's use of drugs, violence, and sexuality, all resulting in a feeling of deep unease among viewers. Of most direct interest is a paragraph describing what King considers the finest scene, the confrontation in the country diner, which King would later reproduce in his own form in "Nona," one of his most disturbing short stories.

16 October 1969: 4, 6 (680 words): By relating his experiences on a picket line attempting to have California grapes removed from the shelves of a local marker, King urges the UMO students to greater political and social awareness, joining the struggle in behalf of Mexican-American laborers whose lives are threatened by pesticides and who live in woefully inadequate housing while the UMO students go to classes and worry about underarm wetness. He concludes with the plea that without responsible action, everything the university stands for becomes "nothing but bullshit."

23 October 1969: 6 (680 words): Changing pace and tone from the previous column, King explores the joys of the World Series, concentrating on the rise of the Mets and concluding that "Baseball's a groove."

30 October 1969: 5 (990 words): Speaking for the NGUSCMC, King puts students on the alert that things are going too well at UMO—there have been no students pelted with eggs, not one demonstration launched against the bookstore, and the football team has actually won a few games. He points to specific individuals responsible for the insidious specter of peace on the campus: Dean Arthur Kaplan, who is consistently fair and thus must be planning something underhanded; David

Bright, editor of the campus newspaper, who actually believes in traditional values; the English faculty, who are organizing such subversive activities as a Poetry Festival (with live poets) and teaching black authors; and President Libby, who, since he is witty, intelligent, articulate, and caring, must also be plotting something—perhaps to give the students a responsible education without their even knowing it. In light of these frightening turns, the "Nitty Gritty etc." plans to take action, beginning with their anticipated assembly of a tactical nuclear weapon to use in bargaining for a more disrupted, less effective University.

6 November 1969: 5 (780 words): In a return to the earlier non-political tone of the "Garbage Truck," King lists the best and worst albums and singles of 1969. On the plus side he includes Bob Dylan's *Nashville Skyline* and the Beatles' *Abbey Road* as albums; the Beatles' "The Ballad of John and Yoko," Simon and Garfunkle's "The Boxer," the Archies' "Sugar Sugar," and Credence Clearwater Revival's "Green River" as singles. The worst albums were *Blood, Sweat, and Tears* ("bad jazz, bad rock, bad lyrics"), George Harrison's *Electronic Music*, and the soundtrack from *Wild in the Streets*; the worst singles Billy Joe Royal's "Cherry Hill Park," Glen Campbell's "Where's the Playground, Susie?" and Blood, Sweat and Tears' "And When I Die."

13 November 1969: 5 (820 words): "The subject this week is cops," King begins, then launches into a defense of the police, outlining the difficulties in working conditions, home life, pay scales, and public opinion that the best officers must endure. He does not ignore the fact that there are bad as well as good; on the whole, however, he finds it to wonder that there are not more bad than there are. Ultimately, the column broadens into a plea for tolerance and understanding—for combatting the tendency to prejudge and classify according to unfair labels.

4 December 1969: 5 (770 words): In another shift of mood, the column indulges in parody and satire of the critical difficulties we face because of clogged urinary tracts. No one drinks water any more, he argues; instead, we drink "milk, beer, chocolate frappes, egg-nogs, Coca-Cola, Pepsi-Cola, RC Cola, root beer, cider, Haig & Haig, Kool-Aid, Za-Rex"—many familiar as brand-name entries in his subsequent fiction. But no one, he points out, drinks water; and the consequences of shifting to water could include world peace and a stronger youth of tomorrow.

11 December 1969: 5 (590 words): In the first annual Trivia contest, King asks questions about television, films, and records, again indicating his abiding interest in the minutiae of contemporary culture.

18 December 1969: 6 (880 words): One of his most intriguing columns, this selection explores the uncanny and inexplicable within the framework of our own world. King refers to unsolved mysteries of history: the disappearance of Judge Crater (an important element in "The Reaper's Image"); UFOs; a rain of frogs in 1936; a troop of Boy Scouts who reported seeing a huge, floating red eye (perhaps an early version of one manifestation of "It"); the disappearance of a Shaker settlement in the 1800s; haunted houses (with a reference to Shirley Jackson's *The Haunting of Hill House* and an oblique glance at *The Shining*); witch cults and mass murders; Joan of Arc, and the Star of Bethlehem. Perhaps there are indeed intersections between our world and other worlds, incomplete at times, that allow for partial transferences. But of course it's all nonsense, he comments periodically through the column until he reaches his conclusion: "Nonsense—but very odd." The column is highly suggestive in light of much of King's later output, themselves explorations of oddities.

8 January 1970: 5 (800 words): The first column of 1970 provides a retrospective on the opening years of the Sixties, with reminiscences of Eisenhower, Churchill, Khrushchev, and the Berlin Wall. Lee Harvey Oswald, Jack Ruby, and James Earl Ray were still unknowns—and King himself was a thirteen-year-old sporting a flat-top haircut, an image made concrete in Reiner's adaptation of "The Body," *Stand by Me*, set in just that period. Between then and the Seventies, too much happened, enough for a century rather than a decade. King specifies certain landmarks of the decade that illustrate the immense changes. In film, the appearance of *The Wild Bunch*, *Bonnie and Clyde*, and *The Graduate*, with their messages of violence and alienation; and the adoption of the G, M, R, X rating codes. "Isolated from our disturbing times," he suggests, "it seems to me that the movies alone contain many indicators of a culture that is going insane." Books carry the same message: *Portnoy's Complaint*, *Go to the Widowmaker*, and *Couples*. Politics reinforces the sense, particularly through the assassinations of the 1960s. And even humor "has taken a sick and angry turn."

15 January 1970: 5 (805 words): After the apocalyptic echoes in the preceding column, King turns to the more collegiate "Last Will and Testament" of a soon-to-graduate senior. The second paragraph acknowledges the UMO English department, and notes that it taught him neither to write nor to read "creatively" and it answered few of his questions in other than generalizations, but it did manage to stay out of his way most of the time. For those services, it (which he capitalizes as "It") receives first mention and his good will and his promise of a glowing letter of recommendation should It decide to relocate to another university. Other beneficiaries include the *Maine Campus*, the UMO Student Senate, and the Maine legislature (he wishes them a "complete change of heart" in fiscal policies), as well as individual students. The columns represents a cross-section of King's attitudes toward politics and politicians, student affairs, social problems, and fads, as well as several heart-felt appreciations for individuals who had impressed him over the years.

5 February 1970: 10 (760 words): King repeats elements of his earlier column on television (6 March 1969), addressing specifically the mid-season replacements beginning in January. He singles out those shows he considers particularly strong: *The Immortal* on ABC, an example of science fiction at its best; *Then Came Bronson*; *Mannix*; *Ironside*; and Pat Paulsen's comedy show. And he lists the weak entries: *The Courtship of Eddie's Father*, *The Flying Nun*, *The Doris Day Show*. He concludes that in spite of its potential, television has grown "wet and sick and fat"; his final paragraph is a direct appeal to the networks that they treat viewers as intelligent human beings rather than as consumers waiting to be huckstered—an attitude that carries over into the fourth Bachman book, *The Running Man*.

12 February 1970: 5 (675 words): In an emotional outburst, King identifies a number of things he is "sick of"—a forerunner to his continuing series of lists of important things that appeared sporadically in *Castle Rock* and elsewhere. Primary among them, he is sick of hearing about the generation gap, about what is wrong with the youth, about what is right with Nixon's "silent majority." The column moves on an emotional, associationalistic level, with King speaking directly to his readership, allowing his anger and frustration to surface: "I don't like it. And I'm not going to have it."

19 February 1970: 8 (650 words): Returning to film criticism, King comments on the Memorial Union Activities Board's lineup of films: *Rosemary's Baby*, *Psycho*, *The Loves of Isidora*, and *The Sand Pebbles*. In addition, MUAB is hosting a film festival including Lugosi's *Dracula*, Karloff's *Frankenstein*, Laughton's *The Hunchback of Notre Dame*, *The Pit and the Pendulum*, and *The Haunting*—the latter among the most frightening films ever made. King's critiques of the films suggest his involvement with the horror film as genre, as well as the immense influence such films would have on his novels and stories; in one sense, the column is a dress rehearsal for his monsters in *IT*.

26 February 1970: 8 (530 words): In another film review, King turns his attention to George Kennedy's performance in ...*tick...tick...tick*, a "racial fairy tale" set in Missouri. King sees the film as tackling weighty issues—treatment of whites and blacks as stereotypes, for example—and praises it for doing so with clarity and humanity.

125

19 March 1970: 5 (690 words): One of King's most impressive short stories is "The Reach," a ghost story set against the backdrop of a New England blizzard; perhaps his most successful (certainly his most teachable) novel is *The Shining*, similarly set for much of the narrative in a Colorado blizzard. In this column, King reprints an unsent letter written just after a blizzard on February 26, 1969. His purpose in writing the letter seems unclear, since it consists primarily of responses to snow and storms. But woven throughout the texture of the letter are images and references that will reverberate through such works as *The Shining*, "The Reach," even in a sense *Christine* and portions of *Misery*. The letter concentrates on King's love-hate relationship with snow, creating a darkly fantastic picture of fingers of snow as they infiltrate The Den, a UMO social center. Bit by bit the artificial lightness of spirit dies as the snow touches each of the twenty students stranded there in a New England, 1970s version of Poe's "The Masque of the Red Death." The image reinforces King's sense of the littleness and fragility of humanity when set against the immenseness of the world (again perhaps an adumbration of the protean monster and its localized havoc in *IT*). Unlike many of his columns, however, King uses this one as a springboard to think about his own writing—his morbidity, his fear of "Things that Lurk," his awareness that "here there be tygers, and we can only catch glimpses of them behind us." This column may be the most stimulating and suggestive of the entire series, since it focuses on a continuing image that King would eventually redefine in his finest works.

26 March 1970: 5 (890 words): King discusses the problem of requirements and required core courses at UMO; his recommendations are that required courses be abolished in favor of closer ties between students and advisor, a suggestion well in keeping with the direction of university curriculum in the late sixties and early seventies.

9 April 1970: 5 (515 words): In another attack on television, King brings in his frustrations with problems at UMO as well, to design a series of television shows modeled on current favorites but adapted to fit UMO personalities: *Nanny and the Professor*, starring a UMO dean who would immediately impose curfews on the kids, daddy, the dog, and the goldfish; *The Courtship of Arthur's Father*, starring yet another dean; *Sing Along with Win*, with UMO President Libby conducting a choir composed of the physical education department, the women faculty members, and a sociology club; *Room 222*, starring the English department; *Security-69* (aka *Adam-12*), starring the UMO security force. There are more possibilities, King concludes, than even he cares to mention.

16 April 1970: 5 (789 words): King outlines the permutations in his political orientation that culminated in his registering as an Independent in 1969. The column focuses on the failings of Republican politics and policies, but even more important are King's rationales for his beliefs. As a "scummy radical bastard," he is constrained by the Declaration of Independence, the Constitution, and the Articles of Confederation to place the individual above the government, which results in one fighting against the draft, opposing a war, deciding for oneself about the morality of drugs or abortion, all without turning over the individual conscience to "Big Brother." King refers as he has done several times to a seminal scene in *Easy Rider*, surely one of the most influential films he mentions in his columns; and he concludes with a plea for individual freedom: each person must decide critical issues alone, without forcing his or her decisions onto anyone else.

30 April 1970: 5 (720 words): In a change of pace, King looks outward, toward spring, and offers some guidelines for professional girl-watching, including a rating system that ranges from 1A ("definitely tops") to 1Z ("Forget it. Pray for rain").

7 May 1970: 5 (960 words): This column is another bellweather column—one of those that indicates so clearly where King has been and where he is heading. In it, he attempts to assess his life to determine "Where We Are At." Beginning in 1953, he recounts his informal education in the facts of American life—that America was always first and right, as witnessed by Randolph Scott in *Gung Ho!* or in war films such as *Halls of Montezuma* and *Sands of Iwo Jima*. Russians were shadowy, threatening figures out there somewhere; Communists were even worse. In 1956, the Hungarian Revolt brought the issue to the open, with King entranced by brave freedom fighters facing the armed might of Russia; after all, Randolph Scott and Richard Widmark and John Wayne had made it clear that all peoples should have their freedom. Then, in 1957, the Russians orbited Sputnik, which was frightening, since Americans were supposed to do everything first, and here the Russians were suddenly ahead (his description of his first hearing about Sputnik, interestingly, differs substantially from that recounted some years later in *Danse Macabre*).[3] In 1960, with Francis Gary Powers, King's faith was again shaken, and shaken again in 1962 when it was revealed that Kennedy had lied about the missile gap. For the first time, he recalls, he felt outright anger against the government.

21 May 1970: 5 (490 words): In the final "Garbage Truck" column, Steve King announces his birth "into the real world," to take place on 5 June 1970. The column is in the form of a birth announcement, beginning with name, date of birth, age, weight, hair and eye color, political views ("extremely radical"), height, complexion ("hairy"), favorite color (blue, although black would be more appropriate in deference to the assassinations of Robert Kennedy, Martin Luther King, the Kent

State students, and the people of My Lai), favorite president (none), favorite University Chancellor (none), favorite films, etc. The list also includes his future prospects: "Hazy, although either nuclear annihilation or environmental strangulation seem to be definite possibilities."

VIII.

THE WORLD-WIDE KING: SOME NOTES ON NON-ENGLISH PUBLICATIONS

King's phenomenal appeal to American readers is well documented; equally phenomenal is his appeal to readers in other nations through foreign publications and foreign-language editions. Full information on such editions is difficult to come by, but even a cursory examination of foreign publications indicates the extent of King's world-wide popularity.

The following is a partial listing of available foreign and foreign-language editions (generally in order of the original English publication date of each major text).

DENMARK: Danish

Drengen der Skinnede [*The Shining*]. Copenhagen: Borgen, 1980.
Cujo: Spaendingsroman. Valby, Denmark: Borgen, 1984.
Dyrekirkegården. Copenhagen, Denmark: Gode Bøger, 1987.

BELGIUM AND THE NETHERLANDS: Dutch[1]

Some of the most dynamic responses to King's fictions have come from the Lowlands: Belgium and the Netherlands. Luitingh, one of the major publishers of King materials, has even distributed a mock-newspaper replete with articles (serious and parodic) about each of the novels it has published; even for readers unfamiliar with Dutch, *Stephen King Krant* is a fascinating document.

Carrie. Utrecht: De Fontein, 1975; Utrecht: Luitingh/Veen, 1983.
Bezeten Stad [*'Salem's Lot*]. Utrecht: Luitingh/Veen, 1978; Utrecht: Skarabee, 1980 [?].
Het Tweede Gezicht [*The Shining*]. Utrecht: De Fontein, 1978.
De Shining. Utrecht: Skarabee, 1983; Utrecht: Luitingh, 1987.
Razernij [*Rage*]. Utrecht: Luitingh, 1988.
De Beproeving [*The Stand*]. Utrecht: Luitingh/Veen, 1984.
It Weet Wat Je Wilt [seven stories from *Night Shift* and *Different Seasons*]. Utrecht: Luitingh/Veen, 1985.
De Satanskindern en Andere Verholen. Utrecht: Luitingh, 1985.
De Laaste Laddersport. Utrecht: Luitingh, 1987.
Dodelijk Dilemma [*The Dead Zone*]. Utrecht: Luitingh, 1980; Utrecht: Skarabee, 1984.
De Marathon [*The Long Walk*]. Utrecht: Luitingh, 1988.
Ogen van Vuur: Firestarter. Utrecht: Luitingh/Veen, 1981, 1986, 1988.

Werk in Uitvoering [*Roadwork*]. Utrecht: Luitingh, 1988.
Cujo. Utrecht: Luitingh/Veen, 1982.
Vlucht Naar de Top [*The Running Man*]. Utrecht: Luitingh, 1988.
Creepshow. Amsterdam: W. L. Beck, 1983
Different Seasons: De Leerling ["Apt Pupil" and "Rita Hayworth and Shaw-shank Redemption"]. Utrecht: Luitingh, 1984, 1988.
De Donkere Toren: I. De Scherpschutter [*The Dark Tower: The Gunslinger*]. Utretch: Luitingh, 1988.
Christine. Utrecht: Luitingh, 1983.
Ogen van de Draak [*The Eyes of the Dragon*]. Utrecht: Luitingh, 1987.
"Kat Uit de Hel" ("The Cat from Hell"), in *Top Horror: De Beste Griezelver-halen Door de Auteurs Zelf Gekozen en Ingeleid* [*Top Horror: The Best Horror Stories, Chosen and Introduced by the Authors Themselves*]. Amsterdam: Loeb, 1985, p. 212-224.
De Talisman. Utrecht: Luitingh/Veen, 1985.
Der Verfloeking [*Thinner*]. Utrecht/Aartselaar: A. W. Bruna and Zoons, 1985.
Duistere Krachten: Verhalen van de Meester van de Horror [stories from *Skeleton Crew*]. Utrecht: Luitingh, 1986, 1988.
Dichte Mist ["The Mist"]. Utrecht: Luitingh, 1986.
Der Spiegelbeeld van de Maaier ["The Reaper's Image"; stories from *Skeleton Crew*]. Utrecht: Luitingh, 1987, 1988.
Silver Bullet: Het Uur van de Weerwolf [*Cycle of the Werewolf*]. Utrecht: Luitingh, 1987.
4 X Stephen King [*The Bachman Books*]. Utrecht: Luitingh, 1986.
Het [*IT*]. Utrecht: Luitingh, 1986.
De Ademhalingsmethode ["The Breathing Method"]. Utrecht: Luitingh, 1987.
De Aap ["The Monkey"]. Utrecht: Luitingh, 1987.
De Ballade van de Flexibele Kogel ["The Ballad of the Flexible Bullet"]. Utrecht: Luitingh, 1987.
Misery. Utrecht: Luitingh, 1987.
De Gloed [*The Tommyknockers*]. Utrecht: Luitingh, 1988.

ENGLAND: English

England is, of course, an immediate source for non-U.S. editions. Many of King's novels and collections have appeared in British editions, occasionally even before the American editions have appeared and often in far more hand-some format than their American counterparts. The covers tend to be more imaginative, and the general production values are usually on a higher level. The hardcover books have slightly different proportions, being narrower and taller than American editions; paper and bindings also tend to be of a higher quality.

At least one dealer/collector has indicated that British editions may become more difficult to locate as a result of agitation for changes in American copyright law; when available, however, the British editions are valuable addi-tions to King collections.

Carrie. London: New English Library, 1974, 1975.
'Salem's Lot. London: New English Library, 1977.
The Shining. London: New English Library, 1977, 1978, 1979.
Rage. London: New English Library, 1983.
The Stand. London: New English Library, 1979, 1980.

The Shining, 'Salem's Lot, Night Shift, Carrie [omnibus edition]. London: Octagon, 1981; London: Heinemann, 1983.

Night Shift. London: New English Library, 1979 [?].

The Dead Zone. London: Macdonald, 1979; London: Futura, 1980; Anstey, Leicestershire: Charnwood, 1983; Leicestershire: Thorpe, 1983.

Firestarter. London: Macdonald Futura, 1980; London: Futura, 1981; Anstey, Leicestershire: Charnwood, 1982.

Roadwork. London: New English Library, 1983.

Danse Macabre. London: Macdonald Futura, 1981; London: Futura, 1981.

Cujo. London: Macdonald, 1982; London: Futura, 1982; Anstey, Leicestershire: Charnwood, 1983.

The Running Man. London: New English Library, 1983.

Different Seasons. London: Macdonald, 1982; London: Futura, 1983.

The Dark Tower: The Gunslinger. London: Sphere, 1988, 1989.

Christine. London: Hodder & Stoughton, 1983; London: New English Library, 1984.

Pet Sematary. London: Hodder & Stoughton, 1984; Bath: Chivers, 1984; London: New English Library, 1985.

The Eyes of the Dragon. London: Macdonald, 1987; Bath: Chivers, 1988; London: Futura, 1988.

The Breathing Method. Bath: Chivers, 1984

The Talisman. London: Viking Penguin, 1984; London: Penguin Books, 1985.

Thinner. London: New English Library, 1985., 1986; Bath: Chivers, 1986.

Skeleton Crew. London: Macdonald, 1985; London: Futura, 1986.

The Bachman Books. London: Hodder & Stoughton, 1986; London: New English Library, 1986, 1987.

IT. London: Hodder & Stoughton, 1986; London: New English Library, 1987.

Misery. London: Hodder & Stoughton, 1987; Bath: Chivers Press, 1988; London: New English Library, 1988.

The Dark Tower II: The Drawing of the Three. London: Sphere, 1988.

The Tommyknockers. London: Hodder & Stoughton, 1988; London: New English Library, 1989.

The Stand: The Complete & Uncut Edition. London: Hodder & Stoughton, 1990.

Four Past Midnight. London: Hodder & Stoughton, 1990; London: New English Library, 1991.

Needful Things. London: Hodder & Stoughton, 1991; London: New English Library, 1994.

Gerald's Game. London: Hodder & Stoughton, 1992.

Dolores Claiborne. London: Hodder & Stoughton, 1993; Sevenoaks, Kent: New English Library, 1993.

Nightmares & Dreamscapes. London: Hodder & Stoughton, 1993.

Insomnia. London: Hodder & Stoughton, 1994; London: New English Library, 1995.

FRANCE: French[2]

Carrie. Paris: Gallimard, 1976; Paris: J'ai-lu/Epouvante, 1978, 1980; Paris: Albin Michel, 1994; Paris: France-Loisirs, 1994.

'Salem's Lot. Paris: Williams-Alta, 1977; Paris: Pocket, 1979; Paris: J. C. Lattes, 1989; Paris: France-Loisirs, 1994.

Rage. Paris: Albin Michel, 1990; Paris: J'ai-lu, 1993; Paris: France-Loisirs, 1994.

Shining, l'Enfant Lumière. Paris: Williams-Alta, 1979; Paris: J'ai-lu/Epouvante, 1981, 1984, 1988; Paris: France-Loisirs, 1991; Paris: J. C. Lattes, 1989, 1992.

Danse Macabre [Night Shift]. Paris: Williams-Alta, 1980; Paris: J'ai-lu/Epouvante, 1982; Paris: J. C. Lattes, 1989, 1993; Paris: France-Loisirs, 1994.

Le Fleau [The Stand]. Paris: J. C. Lattes, 1981; Paris: J'ai-lu, 1988.

Marche ou Crève [The Long Walk]. Paris, Albin Michel, 1989; Paris: J'ai-lu, 1992; Paris: France-Loisirs, 1994.

L'Accident [The Dead Zone]. Paris: J. C. Lattes, 1983; Paris: Le Livre de Poche, 1984; Paris: France-Loisira, 1994.

Charlie [Firestarter]. Paris: Albin Michel, 1984; Paris: J'ai-lu/Epouvante, 1986; Paris: France-Loisirs, 1985.

Chantier [Roadwork]. Paris: Albin Michel, 1987; Paris: J'ai-lu, 1991; Paris: France-Loisirs, 1994.

Cujo. Paris: Albin Michel, 1982; Paris: France-Loisirs, 1984; Paris: J'ai-lu/Epouvante, 1983.

Anatomie de L'Horreur [Stephen King's Danse Macabre]. Paris: Du Rocher, 1995.

Pages Noires [Anatomie de L'Horreur II]. Paris: Du Rocher, 1996.

Creepshow. Paris: Albin Michel/L'Écho des Savanes, 1983.

Running Man [The Running Man]. Paris: Albin Michel, 1988; Paris: France-Loisirs, 1988, 1994; Paris: J'ai-lu, 1989

La Tour Sombre—Le Pistolero [The Dark Tower: The Gunslinger]. Paris: J'ai-lu, 1991; Paris: France-Loisirs, 1994. Individual stories from *The Dark Tower: The Gunslinger* first appeared as: "Le Justicier" ["The Gunslinger"], *Fiction #302* (1979); "Le Relais" ["The Way Station"], *Fiction #317* (1981); "L'Oracle et les Montagnes" ["The Oracle and the Mountains"], *Fiction #327* (1982); "Les Lent Mutants" ["The Slow Mutants"], *Fiction #332* (1982); "Le Justicier et L'Homme en Noir" ["The Gunslinger and the Dark Man"], *Fiction #333* (1982).

Différent Saisons [Different Seasons]. Paris: Albin Michel, 1986; Paris: France-Loisirs, 1986; Paris: J'ai-lu, 1988.

Christine. Paris: Albin Michel, 1984; Paris: France-Loisirs, 1985; Paris: J'ai-lu-Epouvante, 1985.

Simetière [Pet Sematary]. Paris: Albin Michel, 1985; Paris: France-Loisirs, 1986; Paris: J'ai-lu/Epouvante, 1987.

L'Année du Loup-Garou [Cycle of the Werewolf]. Paris: Albin Michel, 1986.

Le Talisman des Territoires [The Talisman, with Peter Straub]. Paris/Lyon: Laffont, 1986; as *Le Talisman*. Paris: Le Livre de Poche, 1987.

Les Yeux du Dragon [The Eyes of the Dragon]. Paris: Albin Michel, 1995.

La Peau sur les Os [Thinner]. Paris: Albin Michel, 1987; Paris: J'ai-lu, 1988; Paris: France-Loisirs, 1994.

Brume: Nouvelles [stories from *Skeleton Crew*]. Paris: Albin Michel, 1987; Paris: France-Loisirs, 1988. *Brume—Paranois [Skeleton Crew*, Book I]. Paris: J'ai-lu, 1989. *Brume—La Faucheuse [Skeleton Crew*, Book II]. Paris: J'ai-lu, 1989.

Nouvelles ["The Monkey" and "Mrs. Todd's Shortcut" in bilingual versions]. Paris: Pocket, 1989.

Le Singe ["The Monkey"]. Paris: Librio, 1994.

La Ballade de la Balle Elastique ["The Ballad of the Flexible Bullet"]. Paris: Librio, 1994.

Peur Bleue [*Silver Bullet*]. Paris: J'ai-lu, 1986; Paris: France-Loisirs, 1994.

Ça [*IT*]. Paris: Albin Michel, 1988; Paris: Albin Michel, 1988 (2 vols); Paris: J'ai-lu, 1990 (3 vols.).

La Tour Sombre—Les Trois Cartes [*The Dark Tower II: The Drawing of the Three*]. Paris: J'ai-lu, 1991; Paris: France-Loisirs, 1994 [omnibus edition].

Miséry. Paris: Albin Michel, 1989; Paris: J'ai-lu, 1991; Paris: France-Loisirs, 1994.

Les Tommyknockers [*The Tommyknockers*]. Paris: Albin Michel, 1989; Paris: France-Loisirs, 1991; Paris: J'ai-lu, 1993 (3 vols.).

Le Part des Ténèbres [*The Dark Half*]. Paris: Albin Michel, 1990; Paris: France-Loisirs, 1991; Paris: Pocket, 1993.

Nouvelles. Paris: Presses Pocket, 1990 (bilingual collection of short fiction).

Le Fleau—Version Integrale [*The Stand: The Complete & Uncut Edition*]. Paris: J. C. Lattes, 1991; Paris: France-Loisirs, 1992; Paris: J'ai-lu, 1992 (3 vols.)

Minuit 2 [*Four Past Midnight*—I]. Paris: Albin Michel, 1991; Paris: France-Loisirs, 1992; Paris: J'ai-lu, 1993.

Minuit 4 [*Four Past Midnight*—2]. Paris: Albin Michel, 1991; Paris: France-Loisirs, 1992; Paris: J'ai-lu, 1994.

La Tour Sombre—Terres Perdues [*The Dark Tower III: The Waste Lands*]. J'ai-lu, 1991; Paris: France-Loisirs, 1994.

Bazaar: Roman [*Needful Things*]. Paris: Albin Michel, 1992; Paris: France-Loisirs, 1993; Paris: J'ai-lu, 1994 (2 vols.).

Jessie [*Gerald's Game*]. Paris: Albin Michel, 1993; Paris: France-Loisirs, 1993; Paris: J'ai-lu, 1996.

Dolores Claiborne. Paris: Albin Michel, 1993; Paris: France-Loisirs, 1994; Paris: Pocket, 1996.

Rêves et Cauchemars [*Nightmares and Dreamscapes*]. Paris: Albin Michel, 1994; Paris: France-Loisire, 1995.

Quelques conseils de Lecture par Stephen King. Paris: Pocket, 1995. [Collection of comments by King, many reprinted as dust-jacket blurbs.]

Insomnie [*Insomnia*]. Paris: Albin Michel, 1995.

La Ligne Verte 1: Deux Petites Filles Mortes [*The Green Mile 1: The Two Dead Girls*]. Paris: Librio, 1996.

La Ligna Verte 2: Mr Jingles [*The Green Mile 2: The Mouse on the Mile*]. Paris: Librio, 1996.

La Ligna Verte 3: Les Mains de Caffey [*The Green Mile 3: Coffey's Hands*]. Paris: Librio, 1996.

La Ligna Verte 4: La Mort Affreuse d'Édouard Delacroix [*The Green Mile 4: The Bad Death of Eduard Delacroix*]. Paris: Librio, 1996.

La Ligna Verte 5 (French title not announced) [*The Green Mile 5: Night Journey*]. Paris: Librio, scheduled for July 1996.

La Ligna Verte 6 (French title not announced) [*The Green Mile 6: Coffey on the Mile*]. Paris: Librio, scheduled for August 1996.

Rosie (tentative title) [*Rose Madder*]. Paris: Albin Michel, scheduled for September 1996.

Desperation (no French title announced). Scheduled for publication by Albin Michel.

The Regulators (no French title announced). Scheduled for publication by Albin Michel.

King's short fiction has also appeared in a number of French publications, including:

Histoires à Lire. Paris: France-Loisirs, 1994. "The Lawnmower Man."

GERMANY, AUSTRIA: German[3]

At least two publishers have printed King's works in German: Bastei-Lübbe (Bergisch Gladbach, Germany) and Wilhelm Heyne (Munich, West Germany). Heyne has the distinction of having produced the only limited edition of *IT*, issued in a print-run of 250 in May, 1986, several months before Viking's American edition; the edition was subsequently challenged for copyright infringement.

The translation of *IT*—appropriately titled simply *ES*—abridges the text from 1138 pages to 860, while remaining as true as possible to the feeling of King's prose. Still, many of the excisions relate directly to King's style. A passage in "Unter der Stadt" ("Under the City"), for example, reads as follows:

"S-S-Seid ihr alle in O-O-Ordnung?" fragte Bill heiser.
"Und du, Bill?" fragte Richie zurück.
"J-J-Ja." Er drehte sich nach Eddie um und drückte ihn fest an sich. "Du hast mir das L-L-Leben gerettet, M-Mann."
"Es hat meinen Schuh gefressen," sagte Eddie, der sich über Bills Worte wahnsinnig freute, aber versuchte, es nicht zu zeigen. "Dieses hundsgemeine blüde Arschloch von Krieschendem Auge!"
"Es had deinen *Schuh* gefressen!" rief Beverly und lachte hysterisch. "Ist das nicht furchtbar schlimm!"
"Ich kauf' dir ein neues Paar, wenn wir wieder draußen sind," sagte Richie. Er klopfte Eddie anerkennend auf den Rücken. "Wie has du das nur gemacht?"
"Ich habe Es mit der Asthmamedizen aus meinem Aspirator beschoßen. So getan, als würe es Süure. So schmeckt das Zeug nach 'ner Weile, wenn ich einen schlechten Tag habe und es oft inhalieren muß. Hat großartig funkionert."
"Na, du solltest ihn wieterhin griffbereit haben," meinte Richie. "Vielleicht brauchen wir ihn noch einmals."
"Ihr habt Es nicht irgenwo gesehen?" fragte Mike. "Als das Streichholz brannte?"
"Es ist w-w-weg," sagte Bill....(*ES*, 772)

The passage contains 183 words. In contrast, the corresponding passage in *IT* (1027-1028) contains 241 words, including references to American brands and fads (Keds and the Mashed Potatoes) and lines important in characterization. Richie's "chucka-licious" and "Eds" disappear, as does an entire paragraph in one of Richie's Voices, along with Eddie's response, "That's the shittiest Voice I ever heard." "Hugged the smaller boy with fierce intensity" becomes "drückte ihn fest an sich" ("held him fast"), while the German text interpolates the comment that Eddie "sich über Bills Worte wahnsinnig freute, aber versuchte, es nicht zu zeigen" ("was insanely happy over Bill's words, but tried not to show it")—a statement unnecessary in the English text. Beverly's suggestion that Eddie keep the aspirator handy is given to Richie in the German text—the only outright error in the passage.

In *ES* the German neuter singular pronoun *es* ("IT") is often used as a proper name, just as King uses it. This avoids what would otherwise be an awkward and irritating problem in German, since *es* regularly changes form as its function in sentences changes. By capitalizing "it," von Reinhardt makes the pronoun into a noun and retains the *ES* form more frequently than one might expect. Occasionally, however, the name quality is lost, as when Eddie urges Bill to attack It; in English, the lines read, "Fight It! You hear me? Fight It, Bill! Kick the shit out of the sucker!" (1026). In *ES*, the form of the pronoun shifts: "Kümpft! Hoert ihr mich? Bekümpf Es, Bill! Gib Ihm einen Tritt, daß die Scheiße nur so aus dem Arschloch rausfliegt!" ("Fight! Do you hear me? Fight It, Bill! Give It a kick, so that the shit flies out of its asshole!") (771). *ES* becomes *Ihm* in the German, however, losing some of the totemic value that King's repetition of "It" creates.

Bill Denbrough's catch-phrase, "He thrusts his fists against the posts and still insists he sees the ghosts," becomes more idiomatically German: "Im finstern Führenwald, da wohnt ein wahrer Meister, der ficht ganz furchtlos kalt sogar noch gegen Geister" ("In the dark Führenwald, there lived a true Master, who fought entirely fearless and cold, even against ghosts"). The rhythm differs from that in King's English version; the phrases are much longer and destroy the driving iambs that emphasize key sibilant sounds—the pattern of iambs and repeated *s*, *st*, and *sts* combinations gives the English line a peculiarly haunting effect, lost in the German. There is little sense that the German phrase would be efficacious as therapy for stuttering. Even the surface meaning shifts radically. The internal function remains the same, however, and von Reinhardt frequently fractures the phrase and intrudes it into sentences and between paragraphs in precisely the way King does, capturing in that way part of King's style.

King's language is lightly censored in *ES* by the substitution of "verflucht" ("accursed"), "verdammt" ("damned"), and other alternatives where King's characters used a harsher, more direct Anglo-Saxon term. The effect is minor, although occasionally some lines are weakened. Bill Denbrough's passionate *"But I don't stutter! I beat it! I DON'T FUCKING STUTTER!"* (*IT* 602) becomes *"Ich hab's überwunden! Verdammt, ich bin kein Stotterer!"* (I've overcome it! Damn, I am not a stutterer!) (*ES* 428). And the translation eliminates entirely Eddie's final line in the paragraph cited from page 1026 of *IT*: *"Jesus Christ you fucking pussies I'm doing the Mashed Potatoes all over It AND I GOT A BROKEN ARM!"*

In spite of these variations, however, *ES* remains true to King's intentions. As the most ambitious German translation, it is a worthwhile effort, giving King's German readership a fine sense of his mastery.

Carrie. München: Frank Schneekluth Verlag, 1977; München: Wilhelm Heyne Verlag, 1977; Bergisch Gladbach: Bastei-Lübbe, 1983, 1987.

Brennen Muß Salem [*'Salem's Lot*]. Vienna, Austria and Hamburg, Germany: Paul Zsolnay, 1979; Munchen: Deutscher Taschenbuchverlag, 1981; Kornwesterheim, Austria: Europäische Bildungsgemeinschaft, 1985; Gütersloh, Austria: Bertelsmann Lesering, 1985, 1986; Vienna, Austria: Buchgemeinschaft Donauland, 1985; Zug, Switzerland: Buch-und-Schallplattenfreunde, 1985; Munchen: Wilhelm Heyne Verlag, 1985.

Shining. Bergisch Gladbach: Bastei-Lübbe, 1980, 1982, 1985; Kornwesterheim, Austria: Europäische Bildungsgemeinschaft, 1985; Gütersloh, Austria: Bertelsmann Lesering, 1985; Vienna, Austria: Buchgemeinschaft Donauland, 1985; Zug, Switzerland: Buch-und-Schallplattenfreunde, 1985; Stuttgart: Deutscher Bücherbund, 1988.

Amok [*Rage*]. München: Wilhelm Heyne Verlag, 1988.

Das Letzte Gefecht [The Stand]. Bergisch Gladback: Bastei-Lübbe, 1985, 1986,1989; Gütersloh, Austria: Bertelsmann Lesering, 1989; Stuttgart: Deutscher Bücherbund, 1989.

Night Shift. Im Morgengrauen. München: Wilhelm Heyne Verlag, 1985. *Katzenauge,* Bergisch Gladbach: Bastei-Lübbe, 1986. *Trucks,* Bergisch Gladbach: Bastei-Lübbe, 1986.

Nachtschicht: Meistererzählungen: Horror bis zum Morgengrauen, Bergisch Gladback, 1987, 1988.

Das Attentat [The Dead Zone]. München: Arthur Moewig Verlag, 1981.

The Dead Zone: Buch zum Film. Rastatt, Germany: Arthur Moewig Verlag, 1984.

Dead Zone: Das Attentat. München: Wilhelm Heyne Verlag, 1987; Gütersloh, Austria: Bertelsmann Lesering, 1988; Stuttgart: Deutscher Bücherbund, 1988.

Todesmarch [The Long Walk]. München: Wilhelm Heyne Verlag.

Feuerkind [Firestarter]. Bergisch Gladbach: Bastei-Lübbe, 1981, 1984; Stuttgart, Germany: Europäische Bildungsgemeinschaft, 1984; Gütersloh, Austria: Bertelsmann Lesering, 1984; Vienna, Austria: Buchgemeinschaft Donauland, 1984; Zug, Switzerland: Buch-und-Schallplattenfreunde, 1984.

Sprengstoff [Roadwork]. München: Wilhelm Heyne Verlag, 1986.

Danse Macabre. München: Wilhelm Heyne Verlag, 1988.

Cujo. Bergisch Gladbach: Bastei-Lübbe, 1983, 1986; Kornwesterheim, Austria: Europäische Bildungsgemeinschaft, 1985; Gütersloh, Austria: Bertelsmann Lesering, 1986; Vienna, Austria: Buchgemeinschaft Donauland, 1986; Zug, Switzerland: Buch-und-Schallplattenfreunde, 1986.

Menschenjagd [The Running Man]. München: Wilhelm Heyne Verlag, 1986.

Creepshow. Bergisch Gladbach: Bastei-Lübbe, 1989.

Frühling, Sommer, Herbst und Tod [Different Seasons]. Bergisch Gladbach: Bastei-Lübbe, 1984.

Jahreszeiten: Herbst und Winter [two selections from *Different Seasons*]. Bergisch Gladbach: Bastei-Lübbe, 1987.

Jahreszeiten: Frühling und Sommer [two selections from *Different Seasons*]. Bergisch Gladbach: Bastei-Lübbe, 1988.

Schwarz [The Dark Tower: The Gunslinger]. München: Wilhelm Heyne Verlag, 1988; Gütersloh, Austria: Bertelsmann Lesering, 1989.

Christine. Bergisch Gladbach: Bastei-Lübbe, 1984; Stuttgart: Europäische Bildungsgemeinschaft, 1985; Gütersloh, Austria: Bertelsmann Lesering, 1985; Vienna, Austria: Buchgemeinschaft Donauland, 1985; Zug, Switzerland: Buch-und-Schallplattenfreunde, 1985.

Das Jahr des Werewolfs [Cycle of the Werewolf]. Bergisch Gladbach: Bastei-Lübbe, 1985. As *Der Werewolf von Tarker Mills [Cycle of the Werewolf]*. Bergisch Gladbach: Bastei-Lübbe Verlag, 1986.

Friedhof der Kuscheltiere [Pet Sematary]. Hamburg: Hoffman & Campe Verlag, 1985. Excerpted in *Der Stern*, 1985. Gütersloh, Austria: Bertelsmann Lesering, 1987; Kornwesterheim, Austria: Europäische Bildungsgemeinschaft, 1987; Gütersloh, Austria: Bertelsmann Lesering, 1987; Vienna, Austria: Buchgemeinschaft Donauland, 1987; Zug, Switzerland: Buch-und-Schallplattenfreunde, 1987; München: Wilhelm Heyne Verlad, 1988; Stuttgart: Deutscher Bücherbund, 1988.

Der Talisman. Hamburg: Hoffman & Campe Verlag, 1986; Stuttgart: Deutscher Bücherband, 1987; Gütersloh, Austria: Bertelsmann Lesering, 1987; München: Wilhelm Heyne Verlag, 1988.

Der Fluch [Thinner]. München: Wilhelm Heyne Verlag, 1985.

Skeleton Crew. Im Morgengrauen: Unheimliche Geschichten. München: Wilhelm Heyne Verlag, 1985. *Nona und die Ratten* ["Nona"]. München: Wilhelm Heyne Verlag, 1985. *Der Gesang der Toten* [stories from *Skeleton Crew*]. München: Wilhelm Heyne Verlag, 1986. *Der Fornit* [stories from *Skeleton Crew*]. München: Wilhelm Heyne Verlag, 1986, 1987.

Nebel ["The Mist"]. Linkenheim, Germany: Edition Phantasia, 1986.

Es [*IT*]. Munchen: Wilhelm Heyne Verlag, 1986, 1989; Gütersloh, Austria: Bertelsmann Lesering, 1986; Kornwesterheim, Austria: Europäische Bildungsgemeinschaft, 1988; Gütersloh, Austria: Bertelsmann Club, 1988; Vienna, Austria: Buchgemeinschaft Donauland, 1988; Zug, Switzerland: Buch-und-Schallplattenfreunde, 1988.

Die Augen des Drachen [*The Eyes of the Dragon*]. München: Wilhelm Heyne Verlag, 1987; Gütersloh, Austria: Bertelsmann Lesering, 1987; Stuttgard: Deutscher Bücherband, 1988.

Todesmarch [*The Long Walk*]. München: Wilhelm Heyne Verlag, 1987.

Sie [*Misery*]. München: Wilhelm Heyne Verlag, 1987; Stuttgart: Deutscher Bücherband, 1988; Kornwesterheim, Austria: Europäische Bildungsgemeinschaft, 1988; Gütersloh, Austria: Bertelsmann Club, 1988; Vienna, Austria: Buchgemeinschaft Donauland, 1988; Zug, Switzerland: Buch-und-Schallplattenfreunde, 1988.

Drei [*The Dark Tower II: The Drawing of the Three*]. München: Wilhelm Heyne Verlag, 1989; Gütersloh, Austria: Bertelsmann Lesering, 1989.

Das Monstrum/Tommyknockers. Hamburg: Hoffman and Campe, 1988.

Nachtgesichter [*Nightmares in the Sky*]. München: Wilhelm Heyne Verlag, 1989; Germany: Droemer/Knaur Verlag, 1989.

Stark [*The Dark Half*]. Hamburg: Hoffman and Campe, 1989; West Germany: Droemer/Knaur Verlag, 1989.

Tot [*The Dark Tower III: The Waste Lands*]. München: Wilhelm Heyne Verlag, 1992.

Schlaflos [*Insomnia*]. München: Wilhelm Heyne Verlag, 1994.

Langoliers [*Four Past Midnight*: "The Langoliers," "Secret Window, Secret Garden"]. München: Wilehlm Heyne Verlag, 1990.

Nachts [*Four Past Midnight*: "The Library Policeman," "The Sun Dog"]. München: Wilhelm Heyne Verlag, 1991.

Das Spiel [*Gerald's Game*]. München: wilhelm Heyne Verlag, 1992.

Alpträume [*Nightmares & Dreamscapes*]. Hamburg: Hoffman & Campe, 1993.

In Einer Kleinen Stadt [*Needful Thimgs*]. Hamburg: Hoffman & Campe, 1991.

Dolores [*Dolores Claiborne*]. Hamburg: Hoffman & Campe, 1992..

Das Bild [*Rose Madder]*. Hamburg: Hoffman & Campe, 1995.

The Green Mile, Teil 1: Der Tod der Jungen Mädchen [*The Green Mile 1: The Two Dead Girls*]. Bergisch Gladbach: Bastei-Lübbe, 1996.

The Green Mile, Teil 2: Die Maus im Todesblock [*The Green Mile 2: The Mouse on the Mile*]. Bergisch Gladbach: Bastei-Lübbe, 1996.

The Green Mile, Teil 3: Coffey's Hände [*The Green Mile 3: Coffey's Hands*]. Bergisch Gladbach: Bastei-Lübbe, 1996.

The Green Mile, Teil 4: Der Qualvolle Tod [*The Green Mile 4: The Bad Death of Eduard Delacroix*]. Bergisch Gladbach: Bastei-Lübbe, 1996.

The Green Mile, Teil 5 [German title not yet announced). Bergisch Gladbach: Bastei-Lübbe, scheduled for 1996.

The Green Mile, Teil 6 [German title not yet announced). Bergisch Gladbach: Bastei-Lübbe, scheduled for 1996.

King's short stories have also appeared in several collections published by Heyne:

Die Grusel Geschichten des Jahres. Stories by King, Dennis Etchison, Ramsey Campbell, and others.
"Twilight Zone": Schatten Licht ("Shadow Light"). Stories by King, Joyce Carol Oates, Robert Bloch, Peter Straub, Thomas Disch, Robert Sheckley, and others.
"Twilight Zone": Daemmer Licht ("Twilight"). Stories by King, Thomas Disch, John Carpenter, Charles L. Grant, Ramsey Campbell, Rod Serling, and others.
"Twilight Zone: Magisches Dunkel ("Magic Darkness"). Stories by King, Peter Straub, Richard Matheson, Ramsey Campbell, Ray Bradbury, Jack C. Haldeman II.

HUNGARY: Hungarian

Dolores Claiborne. Budapest: Europa, 1993.

ICELAND: Icelandic[4]

Duld [*The Shining*]
Reidi [*Rage*]
[*The Dead Zone*]—published in a weekly newspaper
Eldvakinn [*Firestarter*]
Umsatur ["Siege"—*Cujo*]
Visnadu [*Thinner*]
Emyd [*Misery*]
Leikur Geralds [*Gerald's Game*]
Dolores Claiborne [*Dolores Claiborne*]
Midnaeturflug ["Midnight Flight"—"The Langoliers"]
Bokasafnslogreglan (?) ["The Library Policeman"]

ITALY: Italian[5]

Carrie. Milano: Sonzogno, 1977; Milano: Bompiani, 1984, 1987
Notti di Salem [*'Salem's Lot*]. Milano: Sonzogno, 1979.
Shining. Milano: Bompiani, 1978, 1981, 1987.
L'Ombra dello Scorpione [*The Stand*]. Milano: Sonzongo, 1983; Milano: Bompiani, 1985.
Una Splendida Festa di Morte [*Night Shift*]. Milano: Sonzonga, 1978.
La Zona Morta [*The Dead Zone*]. Milano: Sperling & Kupfer, 1981.
La Lunga Marcia: L'Uomo in Fuga [*The Long Walk*]. Milano: Mondadori, 1986.
L'Incendiaria [*Firestarter*]. Milano: Sperling & Kupfer, 1982.
L'Occhio del Male [*Firestarter*]. Milano: Sonzogno, 1986.
Danse Macabre. Italy: Theoria, 1985.
Cujo. Milano: Mondadori, 1983, 1986; Milano: Sperling & Kupfer.
Stagioni Diverse [*Different Seasons*]. Milano: Sperling & Kupfer, 1987.
La Torre Nera: L'Ultimo Cavaliere [*The Dark Tower: The Gunslinger*]. Milano: Sperling & Kupfer.
Christine. Milano: Sperling & Kupfer, 1984.
Unico Indizio: La Luna Piena [*Cycle of the Werewolf*]. Italy: Longanesi, 1986.

Pet Sematary. Milano: Sperling & Kupfer.
Gli Occhi del Drago [*The Eyes of the Dragon*]. Milano: Sperling & Kupfer.
Il Talismano. Milano: Sperling & Kupfer, 1986.
Scheletri. Milano: Sperling & Kupfer.
IT. Milano: Sperling & Kupfer, 1987.
Misery. Milano: Sperling & Kupfer, .
La Torre Nera: La Chiamata Dei Tre [*The Dark Tower II: The Drawing of the Three*]. Milano: Sperling & Kupfer.
Le Creature del Buio [*The Tommyknockers*]. Milano: Sperling & Kupfer.
La Meta Oscura [*The Dark Half*]. Milano: Sperling & Kupfer.
Quattro dopo Mezzanotte [*Four Past Midnight*]. Milano: Sperling & Kupfer.
La Torre Dera: Terre Desolate [*The Dark Tower III: The Waste Lands*]. Milano: Sperling & Kupfer.
Cose Prezioso (L'Ultima Storia di Castle Rock) [*Needful Things*]. Milano: Sperling & Kupfer.
Il Gioco di Gerald [*Gerald's Game*]. Milano: Sperling & Kupfer.

JAPAN: Japanese

Shyainingu [*The Shining*]. Tokyo: Bungei Shunju, 1986.

KOREA: Korean

K'aesullok ui Pinil [*Needful Things*]. Seoul, Toesong, 1992.

NORWAY: Norwegian[6]

Faresonen [*Cujo*]. Oslo: Hjemmets Bokklubb.
Ildbarnet [*Firestarter*]. Oslo: Hjemmets Bokklubb.
Morke Krefter [*The Dead Zone*]. Oslo: Hjemmets Bokklubb.
Ondskapens Hotel [*The Shining*]. Norway: Fredhois verlag.
Dolores Claiborne. Norway: H. Aschebourg.
Insomnia. Norway: H. Aschebourg.

POLAND: Polish

Gra Geralda [*Gerald's Game*]. Waeszawa: Prima, 1994.

RUSSIA and UKRAINE: Russian[7]

Firestarter/The Mist. St. Petersburg: Neva-Lad, 1992.[8]
The Shining/"Apt Pupil." St. Petersburg: Neva-Lad, 1992.
The Shining. Moscow: Cadman, 1992
Misery. St. Petersburg: IMA-Press-Advertising, 1992.
Quarter Past Midnight [*Four Past Midnight*]. St. Petersburg, IMA-Press-Advertising, 1993.
Bloody Games [*Pet Sematary* and *The Eyes of the Dragon*]. St. Petersburg: IMA-Press-Advertising, 1993.
Damnation of the Underground Ghosts [*The Tommyknockers*]. St. Petersburg: IMA-Press-Advertising, 1993.
The Dark Half [*The Dark Half*, " Graveyard Shift," and "I am the Doorway"]. Moscow: Cadman, 1993.
'Salem's Lot [*'Salem's Lot,* "Cain Rose Up, "The Reaper's Image"]. Moscow: Cadman, 1993.

Thinner ["The Body" and *Thinner*]. Moscow: Cadman, 1993.
Cujo [*Cujo*, "Rita Hayworth and Shawshank Redemption," "Gramma," and "Mrs. Todd's Shortcut"]. Moscow: Cadman: 1993.
Armageddon: Book I [*The Stand: The Complete & Uncut Edition*]. Moscow: Cadman, 1993.
Christine. Moscow: Cadman, 1993.
The Running Man [*The Running Man*, "The Breathing Method," "Popsy," "The Lawnmower Man," "Night Surf," "The Man Who Loved Flowers," "The Woman in the Room," and "I Know What You Need"]. Moscow: Cadman, 1993.
IT. Moscow: Cadman, 1993, 2 vols.
Neobkhodimye Veshchi: Poslednaia Naibolee Polnaia Istoriia Kastl Roka [*Needful Things*]. L'vov, Ukraine: Khronos, 1993.
Nightmares and Dreamscapes. Moscow: Mir, 1994.
The Talisman. Moscow: Cadman, 1994.
The Dead Zone [*The Dead Zone*, "Secret Window, Secret Garden," "The Library Policeman"]. L'vov, Ukraine: Sigma, 1994.
Dolores Claiborne [*Gerald's Game* and *Dolores Claiborne*]. L'vov, Ukraine: Sigma, 1995.
The Long Walk [*The Long Walk*, "Dolan's Cadillac," "Dedication," "Sneakers," "The End of the Whole Mess"]. L'vov: Sigma, 1995.
Rage [*Rage*, "Suffer the Little Children," "You Know They Got a Hell of a Band," "The Moving Finger," "Chattery Teeth," "The Night Flier," "The Wedding Gig"]. L'vov, Ukraine: Sigma, 1995.
Roadwork. L'vov, Ukraine: Sigma, 1995.
The Dark Tower Series [*The Dark Tower: The Gunslinger* and *The Dark Tower II: The Drawing of the Three*]. Kharkov, Ukraine: Delta.
The Dark Tower Series [*The Dark Tower III: The Waste Lands*]. Kharkov, Ukraine: Delta, 1995.
Insomnia. Kharkov, Ukraine, 1995.
Rose Madder. Kharkov, Ukraine: Delta.
Dolores Kleiborn; Mizori: Romany [*Dolores Claiborne* and *Misery*]. L'vov, Ukraine: Kameniar, 1995.
The Eyes of the Dragon. Kharkov, Ukraine: Polygraphbook.
Apt Pupil ["Apt Pupil," "Rainy Season," "The Ten-O'Clock People,""Crouch End," "The House on Maple Street," "My Pretty Pony," "Home Delivery," "The Fifth Quarter," "It Grows on You," "Sorry, Right Number," "The Ledge"]. L'vov, Ukraine: Sigma, 1995.
Carrie [*Carrie*, "Umney's Last Case," "Cycle of the Werewolf," "The Last Rung on the Ladder"]. L'vov, Ukraine: Sigma, 1995.
The Waste Lands. L'vov, Ukraine: Sigma, 1995.

Michael McAlcin has posted computer scans of covers for a number of Russian translations of King's work, along with bibliographical information, on the internet.

SPAIN, MEXICO, ARGENTINA, PANAMA, THE UNITED STATES: Spanish

Carrie. Barcelona: Pomaire, 1975, 1978, 1981; Barcelona: Círculo de Lectores, 1978; Barcelona: Plaza & Janés, 1985, 1989; Barcelona: Laertes, 1988.
Hora del Vampiro [*'Salem's Lot*]. Barcelona: Pomaire, 1976; Barcelona: Círculo de Lectores, 1978. As: *El Misterio de 'Salem's Lot*. Barcelona:

Plaza y Janés, 1985, 1987, 1989. As: *La Hora del Vampiro*, Buenos Aires, Argentina: Emece, 1986 [?].

Insolito Esplendor [The Shining]. Barcelona: Pomaire, 1978, 1981; Barcelona: Círculo de Lectores, 1979; Barcelona, Plaza & Janés, 1982, 1986, 1987, 1989.

Rabia [Rage]. Barcelona: Martínez Roca, 1987.

El Umbral de la Noche [Night Shift]. Barcelona: Pomaire, 1979; Barcelona: Plaza y Janés, 1985, 1989.

La Zona Muerta [The Dead Zone]. Barcelona: Pomaire, 1981; Barcelona: Mundo Actual de Ediciones, 1981; Panamá: Printer Internacional de Panamá, 1982; Barcelona: Plaza y Janés, 1985, 1986, 1989; Buenos Aires, Argentina: Emece, 1986 [?]; Cuidad de México: Edivisión, 1986.

La Larga Marcha [The Long Walk]. Barcelona: Martínez Roca, 1986.

Ojos de Fuego [Firestarter]. Barcelona: Pomaire, 1981; Panamá: Printer Internacional de Panamá, 1982; Barcelona: Mundo Actual de Ediciones, 1982; Barcelona: Plaza y Janés, 1985, 1987, 1989; Buenos Aires, Argentina: Emece, 1986.

Carretera Maldita [Roadwork]. Barcelona: Martínez Roca, 1987.

La Danza de la Muerte. Barcelona: Plaza y Janés, 1986, 1989.

Cujo. Barcelona: Grijalbo, 1982; Miguel Hidalgo, México: Grijalbo, 1983; Panamá: Printer Internacional de Panamá, 1983; Barcelona: Grijalbo, 1986, 1989.

El Fugitivo [The Running Man]. Barcelona: Martínez Roca, 1986; Barcelona: Círculo de Lectores, 1987.

Different Seasons. Verano de Corrupción. Barcelona: Grijalbo, 1983, 1986, 1989. *El Cuerpo.* Barcelona: Grijalbo, 1983, 1987. *Verano de Corrupción: El Cuerpo.* Barcelona: Mundo Actual de Ediciones, 1984.

Christine. Barcelona: Plaza y Janés, 1983; México: Edivisión, 1984; Panamá: Printer Internacional de Panamá, 1984; Buenos Aires, Argentina: Emece, 1984.

El Ciclo del Hombre Lobo [Cycle of the Werewolf]. Barcelona: Planeta, 1986.

Cementerio de Animales [Pet Sematary]. Barcelona: Plaza y Janés, 1984, 1987, 1989; Buenos Aires, Argentina: Emece, 1984. As: *Cemetario de Mascotas.* México: Edivisión, 1985; Valencia: Círculo de Lectores, 1986.

Los Ojos del Dragon [Eyes of the Dragon]. Buenos Aires, Argentina: Emece Editores, 1987; Barcelona: Plaza y Janés, 1988, 1989; Barcelona: Círculo de Lectores, 1989.

El Talisman. Barcelona: Planeta, 1984.

Maleficio [Thinner]. Buenos Aires, Argentina: Emece Editores, 1986; Barcelona: Plaza y Janés, 1986, 1989; Barcelona: Círculo de Lectores, 1989.

Skeleton Crew. La Niebla ["The Mist"]. Barcelona: Grijalbo, 1986. *La Expedición* [stories from *Skeleton Crew*]. Barcelona: Grijalbo, 1987. *Historias Fantásticas* [stories from *Skeleton Crew*]. Barcelona: Plaza y Janés, 1989; Madrid: Plaza Jovan, 1989. *La Larga Marcha.* Barcelona: Martínez Roca, 1986; Barcelona: Círculo de Lectores, 1987.

Eso [IT]. Barcelona: Plaza y Janés, 1987, 1989.

Misery. Barcelona: Plaza y Janés, 1989.

Los Tommyknockers. Barcelona: Plaza y Janés, 1989.

La Mitad Siniestra [The Dark Half]. México, D.F.: Editorial Grijalbo, 1990.

Apocalipsis [The Stand: The Complete & Uncut Edition]. Barcelona: Plaza y Janés, 1990.

La Tienda [Needful Things]. Barcelona: Ediciones B, 1992.

La Tienda de los Deseos Malignos [*Needful Things*]. México: Grijalbo, 1992.
El Juego de Gerald [*Gerald's Game*]. México, D.F.: Editorial Grijalbo, 1993.
Dolores Claiborne. México, D.F.: Editorial Grijalbo, 1993; Barcelona, Spain: Ediciones B, 1993.
Los Langoliers. New York: Signet, 1995.

SWEDEN: Swedish[9]

Carrie. Stockholm: Askild and Kärnekull, 1980.
Staden Som Försvann [*'Salem's Lot*]. Stockholm: Legenda, 1985.
Varsel [*The Shining*]. Stockholm: Askild and Kärnekull, 1980, 1981, 1983.
Pestens Tid [*The Stand*]. Höganäs: Bra Böcker, 1988; Stockholm, Legenda, 1988.
Raseri [*Rage*]. Stockholm, Legenda; Höganäs: Bra Böcker, 1987.
Dödsbädden [*Night Shift*]. Stockholm: B. Wahlström, 1985, 1987.
Död Zon [*The Dead Zone*]. Stockholm: Askild and Kärnekull, 1983.
Maratonmarschen [*The Long Walk*]. Stockholm: Legenda, 1987.
Eldfödd [*Firestarter*]. Stockholm: Askild and Kärnekull, 1981.
Vägbygge [*Roadwork*]. Höganäs: Bra Böcker, 1988; Stockholm: Legenda, 1988.
Dödsdansen [*Stephen King's Danse Macabre*]. Sweden: Wahlströms, 1991.
Cujo. Stockholm: Askild and Kärnekull, 1982; Stockholm: Legenda, 1985.
Den Flyende Mannen [*The Running Man*]. Stockholm: Legenda, 1986.
Creepshow [*Creepshow*]. Sweden: Smilax, 1991.
Different Seasons. *Sommerdod: Twa Berättelser*. Stockholm: Askild and Kärnekull, 1983. *Vinterverk: Tva Berättelser*. Stockholm: Askild and Kärnekull, 1984.
Det Svarta Tornet Del 1—Revolvermannen [*The Dark Tower: The Gunslinger*]. Stockholm: Legenda, 1989.
Christine. Stockholm: Legenda, 1985, 1987.
Varulvans År [*Cycle of the Werewolf*]. Stockholm: B Wahlström, 1986.
Jurtiyrkogården [*Pet Sematary*]. Höganäs: Bra Böcker, 1984; Stockholm: Legenda, 1986.
Drakens Ögon [*The Eyes of the Dragon*]. Stockholm: Legenda, 1988.
Talismann. Höganäs: Bra Böcker, 1987. As: *Taliemanen*. Stockholm: Legenda/Norstadt, 1988.
Förbannelse [*Thinner*]. Stockholm: Legenda, 1986. 1988; Höganäs: Bra Böcker, 1987.
Den Förskräcklinga Apan och Andra Berättelser [stories from *Skeleton Crew*]. Stockholm: Legenda, 1986, 1987.
Det [*IT*]. Stockholm: Legenda, 1987, 1988
Lida [*Misery*]. Stockholm: Legenda, 1988; Höganäs: Bra Böcker, 1988.
Det Svarta Tornet Del 2—Följeslagarna [*The Dark Tower II: The Drawing of the Three*]. Stockholm: Legenda, 1990.
Knackarna [*The Tommyknockers*]. Stockholm: Legenda, 1989.
Stark [*The Dark Half*]. Stockholm: Legenda, 1990.
Pestins Tid—Den Oavkortade Versionen [*The Stand: The Complete & Uncut Edition*]. Stockholm: Legenda, 1995.
Mardrömmar [*Four Past Midnight*]. Stockholm, Legenda, 1991.
Köplust [*Needful Things*]. Stockholm, Legenda, 1992.
Dolores Claiborne [*Dolores Claiborne*]. Stockholm, Legenda, 1993.
Geralds Lek [*Gerald's Game*]. Stockholm: Legenda, 1994.
Sömnlös [*Insomnia*]. Höganäs: Bra Böcker, 1996.

Rasande Rose [*Rose Madder*]. Höganäs: Bra Böcker, 1996.

YUGOSLAVIA and CROATIA

Vidovitost [*The Shining*]. Mladost Zagreb, 1981.

NOTE: More complete publication information on foreign and foreign-language editions can be found in Michael R. Collings's *The Work of Stephen King: An Annotated Bibliography & Guide* (San Bernardino, CA: Borgo Press, 1996).

NOTES

CHAPTER I

[1]Stephen King, "Stephen King Comments on *IT*," in *Castle Rock: The Stephen King Newsletter* (July 1986): 5.

[2]Michael R. Collings, *The Many Facets of Stephen King* (Mercer Island WA: Starmont House, 1985), p. 67.

[3]Stephen King, "Stephen King Comments on *IT*," p. 5.

[4]Michael R. Collings and David A. Engebretson, *The Shorter Works of Stephen King* (Mercer Island WA: Starmont House, 1985), p. 145-146.

[5]Letter to Michael R. Collings. March 3, 1986.

[6]Alex E. Alexander, "Stephen King's *Carrie*: A Universal Fairy Tale," in *Journal of Popular Culture* (Fall 1979): 282-288.

[7]Chelsea Quinn Yarbro, "Cinderella's Revenge: Twists on Fairy Tale and Mythic Themes in the Work of Stephen King," in *Fear Itself: The Horror Fiction of Stephen King*, edited by Tim Underwood and Chuck Miller (San Francisco, CA: Underwood-Miller, 1982), p. 63-73.

[8]Letter to Michael R. Collings. March 3, 1986.

[9]Stefan Kanfer (with Cathy Booth), "King of Horror," in *Time* (October 6, 1986): 83.

[10]Letter to Michael R. Collings. March 31, 1986.

CHAPTER II

[1]The original version of this essay appeared in *Castle Rock* 3:11 (November 1987): 1, 4-5.

[2]Editor's column, *Castle Rock* (September 1987): 5.

[3]It is interesting to note that the subsequent made-for-television film version undercut King's fundamental premise, substituting physical aliens, revenants brought to life by vampirizing human energy.

[4]*The Tommyknockers* touches on this critical theme, of course, particularly in introducing Ruth McCausland (222-224), and in discussing Haven's reactions to Jim Gardener (289); but it does not make it the central issue of the novel.

[5]Michael R. Collings, "*The Stand*: Science Fiction into Fantasy," in *Discovering Stephen King*, ed. Darrell Schweitzer (Mercer Island WA: Starmont House, 1985), p. 83-90.

[6]*Danse Macabre* (New York: Everest House, 1981), 16-17.

[7]In *Dolores Claiborne*, King transforms his "monstrous woman" motif into something resembling an Earth-mother icon, as powerful and as threatening as the earlier versions, but now placed in a context that allows Dolores Claiborne to risk all to save her child.

CHAPTER III

[1]A substantially shorter version of this chapter appeared as "The Bestselling Bestseller: King and the Lists," in *Castle Rock: The Stephen King Newsletter* (October 1986): 1, 3. It included much of the material included in the opening pages of this chapter, deleting the listing of weekly appearances on bestsellers' lists.

[2]Goldstein, Bill, "King of Horror," in *Publishers Weekly* (January 24, 1991): 6-9. Goldstein placed the number at 89,000,000 as of the end of 1990; since then, *Four Past Midnight* alone tallied over 3,000,000 copies.

[3]Karen Hinckley and Barbara Hinckley, *American Best Sellers: A Reader's Guide to Popular Fiction* (Bloomington and Indianapolis: Indiana University Press, 1989), p. 222.

[4]Richard Hendricks, "King Publishing Empire for 1992," 26 March 1993 (Netscape, 26 June 1996). Available at: http://phrtay10.ucsd.edu/ed/sk/money_1992.html.

[5]Daisy Maryles, "Hardcover Bestsellers: These Were the Year's BIG Sellers," in *Publishers Weekly* (14 March 1986): 29-31.

CHAPTER IV

[1]Loukia Louka, "Horror Stories Have Staying Power: The Dispatch Talks with Stephen King," in *Maryland Coast Dispatch* (August 8, 1986): 86.

[2]Stephen Beeber, "Stephen King: On the Dark Side with the Master of Horror" (Atlanta, GA, July 19, 1986): 16-A.

[3]Susin Shapiro, "One Picture Is Worth a Million Words," in [New York] *Daily News Magazine* (July 13, 1986): 10.

[4]Shapiro, p. 10.

[5]Larry Ratliff, "Stephen King's *Maxmum Overdrive* Spins Its Wheels," [San Antonio, TX], 1986.

[6]Robert Garrett, "'Overdrive': Bodies by King," in *Boston Globe* (July 26, 1986).

[7]Louka, p. 11.

[8]Michael Burkett, "Schockmeister: King Takes a Run at Directing," in *The Orange County Register* (July 20, 1986): H1.

[9]Stephen Holden, "At the Movies: Rob Reiner Films Unusual Teen Drama," in *New York Times* (August 8, 1986): C8.

[10]Daniel Cziraky, "'Body' Praised," in *Castle Rock: The Stephen King Newsletter* (October 1986): 8.

[11]Rex Reed, "'Stand by Me'—A Corny Kids' Caper," in *New York Post* (August 8, 1986): 22.

[12]Kevin Lally, "Here's a Movie to Stand By: Stephen King Adaptation a Sleeper," in *The Courier-News* [Bridgewater, NJ] (August 8, 1986): C1.

[13]Stephen King, Letter to Michael R. Collings. March 31, 1986.

[14]Holden, p. C8.

[15]Richard Freedman, "Boys Will Be Boys in Refreshing 'Stand by Me,'" in *The Star-Ledger* [Newark, NJ] (August 8, 1986): 49.

[16]Sheila Benson, "Stand by Me," in *Los Angeles Times* (August 31, 1986): 27.

[17]Tom Cuneff, "Stand by Me," in *People* (September 1, 1986): 12.

[18]David Brooks, "What Is Death? What Is Goofy?" in *Insight* (September 1, 1986): 57.

[19]Robert Hunt, "King of Horror," *St. Louis* (August 1986): 40

20Hunt, p. 40-42.

21Jack Sullivan, "Ten Ways to Write a Gothic," in *New York Times Book Review* (February 20, 1977): 8.

22Michael Mewshaw, "Novels and Stories," in *New York Times Book Review* (March 26, 1978): 13+.

23John Podhoretz, "Stopping 'It' Before It's Too Late," in *Insight* (August 25, 1986): 68.

24Stephen King, "Love Those Long Novels," in *Adelina* (November 1980): 9.

25Stephen King, Letter to Michael R. Collings, March 31, 1986.

26Stephen King, Letter to Michael R. Collings, March 3, 1986.

27Podhoretz, p. 69.

28Whoppi Goldberg, "It," in *Los Angeles Times Book Review* (October 2, 1986): 2.

29Beeber, p. 16A.

30Douglas E. Winter, "John Coyne: A Profile," in *Fantasy Review* (October 1985): 13-14.

31James Egan, "'A Single Powerful Spectacle': Stephen King's Gothic Melodrama," in *Extrapolation* (Spring 1986): 74.

32Gary K. Wolfe, "Strange Invaders: An Essay-Review," *Modern Fiction Studies* (Spring 1986): 148.

33Gary Crawford, "Criticism," in *The Penguin Encyclopedia of Horror and the Supernatural*, edited by Jack Sullivan (New York: Viking, 1986), p. 103.

34Wolfe, p. 147-148.

35*Fantasy Review* (June 1984): 10-12.

36Christopher Spruce, "Stephen King: The Critics' Non-Choice," in *Castle Rock: The Stephen King Newletter* (December 1985): 1+.

37Spruce, p. 4.

CHAPTER V

1An earlier version of this chapter appeared as "Of Books and Reputations: The Confusing Cases of King, Koontz, and Others," in *Demon-Driven: Stephen King and the Art of Writing*, edited by George Beahm (Williamsburg, VA: GB Publishing/Ink, 1994), p. 5-11; the original essay was subsequently reprinted in *The Stephen King Companion, Revised Edition*, edited by George Beahm (Kansas City, MO: Andrews and McMeel, 1995).

2"Banned Books Online," Carnegie-Mellon University. Netscape, 1995.

CHAPTER VI

1The earliest version of this essay was presented as the Author Guest of Honor at "Horrorfest '89," on May 13, 1989 in Estes Park Co. The conference was held at the Stanley Hotel, the original inspiration for King's Overlook Hotel in *The Shining*. That version was subsequently published in *Castle Rock: The Stephen King Newsletter* 5:8 (August, 1989): 1, 8; 5:9-10 (September-October, 1989): 3, 10.

2See, for instance, Shawn Hutson's *Slugs* and *The Breeding Ground* for examples of mindless horror that simply continues from one novel to the next. The tendency for horror novels and films to spawn sequels (*i.e.*, *Halloween*, *Nightmare on Elm Street*, *The Fly*, even *The Lawnmower Man II*, etc.) also suggests King's independence and originality. Although characters and locales recur—particularly in the complex interlinkings associated with Dark Tower motifs in the Dark Tower series, *The Stand*, *The Eyes of the Dragon*, and *Insomnia*—King has yet to write a clear sequel, although he has in the past made comments about continuing *'Salem's Lot*.

[3]This same column also twice refers explicitly to the line, "here there be Tygers," another cross-connection with that early story.

[4]*Skeleton Crew* (New York: Putnam, 1985), p. 499.

[5]*Skeleton Crew*, p. 504.

[6]*The Dark Tower: The Gunslinger* (1982; New York: New American Library/Plume, 1988), p. 12.

[7]*The Stand* (New York: Doubleday, 1978), p. 126; *The Stand: The Complete & Uncut Edition* (New York: Doubleday, 1990), p. 184

[8]*The Stand*, p. 124; *Complete & Uncut Edition*, p. 182. The latter alters slightly a single phrase in the passage: "turning away of countenance."

[9]*The Stand*, p. 123; *The Complete & Uncut Edition*, p. 182.

CHAPTER VII

[1]Stefan Kanfer (with Cathy Booth), "King of Horror," in *Time* (October 6, 1986): 77.

[2]Stephen King, *The Stand: The Complete & Uncut Edition* (New York: Doubleday, 1990), p. 226-228.

[3]Michael R. Collings, *The Many Facets of Stephen King* (Mercer Island, WA: Starmont House, 1985), p. 23-25.

CHAPTER VIII

[1]Eddy C. Bertin provided an excellent descriptive bibliography of translations in Belgium and The Netherlands for *Castle Rock* in 1985; over the next few months, he sent several updates.

[2]Much of the data on French-language editions was provided or verified by Hugues Morin in an E-mail message to Michael R. Collings, 23 June 1996.

[3]Much of the data for German editions 1990-1996 was supplied or verified by Lars Jedinski, E-mail message to Michael R. Collings, 27 June 1996.

[4]Information on Icelandic translations was based on an E-mail message from Arnar Freyr Gudmundsson to Michael Collings, 1 July 1996.

[5]Information on Italian translations was augmented and verified by Andrea Masera, a representative of Sperling & Kupfer, in an E-mail message to Michael R. Collings, 22 June 1996.

[6]In May 1984, Tom Egeland wrote to Stephen King, enclosing a copy of Egeland's article for the Norwegian paper *Aftenposten*, and providing a list of the King novels that had then been translated into Norwegian.

[7]Data on Russian editions was supplied by Michael Yu. McAlcin of Moscow, Russia. In an E-mail message to Michael R. Collings, 22 June 1996, he notes that many if not all of the Russian editions may be illegal; when asked to translate *The Green Mile 1*, McAlcin declined. Titles published by Sigma and Delta are Ukrainian publications; all others are Russian.

[8]In a number of cases, several of King's works—novels as well as short fiction—have been collected and published under a single title, often with little apparent justification for the combinations. Because of this approach, I have listed the books by year as they appeared in Russian. Where known, the Russian title has been translated literally into English.

[9]Swedish publication data was supplied and/or verified by Hans-Ake Lilja in an E-mail message to Michael R. Collings, 27 June 1996.

SELECTED BIBLIOGRAPHY

Ahlgren, Calvin. "King of Horror Finds Directing Unnerving." *San Francisco Chronicle* (27 July, 1986).

Alexander, Alex E. "Stephen King's *Carrie*: A Universal Fairy Tale." *Journal of Popular Culture* (Fall 1979): 282-288.

Anker, Roger. "An Artist's Profile: Stephen Gervais." *Fantasy Review* (October 1985): 9-11.

Ansen, David. "Growing Up in the Fifties: Two Coming of Age Films Explore the Way We Were." *Newsweek* 25 (August, 1986): 63.

Beahm, George, ed. *Demon-Driven: Stephen King and the Art of Writing.* Williamsburg VA: GB Publishing/Ink, 1994.

___, ed. *The Stephen King Companion.* Kansas City, MO: Andrews and McMeel, 1989.

___, comp. *The Stephen King Companion*, rev. and enlarged edition. Kansas City, MO: Andrews and McMeel, 1995.

Beale, Lewis. "The King of Horror: The Author of *Carrie* and *The Shining* Takes a Stab at Directing." *Los Angeles Daily News* (24 July 1986); *The Press-Enterprise* (Riverside CA) (24 July 1986): F5.

Beeber, Steven. "Stephen King: On the Dark Side with the Master of Horror." Atlanta GA, 19 July 1986.

Benson, Sheila. "*Stand by Me.*" Los Angeles *Times* "Calendar" (31 August 1986): 27.

Bertin, Eddy C. "Stephen King in the Lowlands." *Castle Rock* (November, 1985): 7-8.

___. Additions to "Stephen King in the Lowlands." Manuscript, 1986.

Bleiler, E. F. "Books." *Twilight Zone Magazine* (February, 1987): 8-11, 43.

Brooks, David. "What Is Death, What Is Goofy?" *Insight* 1 (September, 1986): 57.

Burkett, Michael. "Full Throttle with Stephen King." *New Times* (Phoenix, AZ) (30 July 1986): 79, 83-84. Unexpurgated version of "Shockmeister," differing primarily in the phrasing of the final line.

___. "Shockmeister: King Takes a Run at Directing." *The Orange Country Register* (CA) (20 July 1986): H1-H2.

Carroll, Kathleen. "And Along the Way, They All Grow Up." New York *Daily News* (8 August 1986): 3.

Chevannes, Ingrid, and Dermot McEvoy, "Mass Market Paperbacks." *Publishers Weekly* (March 8, 1991): 28-29.

Clark, Mike. "'Stand by Me' Is a Summer Standout." *USA Today* (8 August 1986).

Collings, Michael R. *The Annotated Guide to Stephen King: A Primary and Secondary Bibliography of the Works of America's Premier Horror Writer.* Mercer Island, WA: Starmont House, 1986.

___. "*The Stand:* Science Fiction into Horror," in *Discovering Stephen King*, edited by Darrell Schweitzer. Mercer Island, WA: Starmont House, 1985, 83-90.

___. *The Films of Stephen King*. Mercer Island, WA: Starmont House, 1986.
___. "*IT*: Stephen King's Comprehensive Masterpiece." *Castle Rock* (July, 1986): 1, 4-6.
___. *The Many Facets of Stephen King*. Mercer Island, WA: Starmont House, 1985.
___. *Stephen King as Richard Bachman*. Mercer Island, WA: Starmont House, 1985.
___. *The Work of Stephen King: An Annotated Bibliography & Guide*. Edited by Boden Clarke. BIBLIOGRAPHIES OF MODERN AUTHORS, No. 25. San Bernardino, CA: Borgo Press, 1996.
Collings, Michael R., and David A. Engebretson. *The Shorter Works of Stephen King*. Mercer Island, WA: Starmont House, 1985.
Corliss, Richard. "No Slumming in Summertime: Three Ambitious Films Enliven the Dog Days." *Time* (25 August 1986): 62.
Crawford, Gary. "Criticism." *The Penguin Encyclopedia of Horror and the Supernatural*, ed. Jack Sullivan. New York: Viking, 1986: 101-103.
Cuneff, Tom. "Stand by Me." *People* (1 September 1986): 12.
Cziraky, Daniel. "'Body' Praised." *Castle Rock* (October, 1986): 8.
Delany, Samuel R. "Some Reflections on SF Criticism." *Science Fiction Studies* (November, 1981): 233-239.
___. "Generic Protocols: Science Fiction and the Mundane." *The Technological Imagination: Theories and Fictions*, ed. Theresa de Laurentiis, Andreas Huyssen, and Kathleen Woodward. Madison, WI: Coda, 1980: 175-193.
Duiz, Roberto. "Stephen King: Horror." *Lui* (July/August 1986): 108-109.
Egan, James. "Antidetection: Gothic and Detective Conventions in the Fiction of Stephen King." *Clue: A Journal of Detection* 5 (1984): 131-46.
___. "Apocalypticism in the Fiction of Stephen King." *Extrapolation* (Fall, 1984): 214-227.
___. "'A Single Powerful Spectacle: Stephen King's Gothic Melodrama." *Extrapolation* (Spring, 1986): 62-75.
Egeland, Tom. "Morkets Meister." *Aftenposten* (Oslo, Norway) (18 April, 1984).
Fleming, Richard. "Prince of Darkness: Q & A with Stephen King." *LA Free Weekly Reader* (1 August 1986): 10.
Floyd, Jonathan. "Stephen King Is Scaring Me." *Grue* #2 (1986): 53-62.
Freedman, Richard. "Boys Will Be Boys in Refreshing 'Stand by Me.'" *The Star-Ledger* (Newark, NJ) (8 August 1986): 49.
Garrett, Robert. "'Overdrive': Bodies by King." *Boston Globe* (26 July 1986).
Gates, David. "The Creature That Refused to Die." *Newsweek* (1 September 1986): 84. Review of *IT*.
Gibbs, Kenneth. "Stephen King and the Tradition of American Gothic." *Gothic* 1 (1986): 6-14.
Goldberg, Whoopi. "It." *The Book Review* (*Los Angeles Times*) (2 October 1986): 2.
Goldstein, Bill. "King of Horror." *Publishers Weekly* (24 January 1991): 6-9.
Goodman, Walter. "Film: Rob Reiner's 'Stand by Me': A Walk into the Past." *New York Times* (8 August 1986): C10.
Gundmundsson, Arnar Freyr. E-mail message to Michael R. Collings. 1 July 1996.
Hinckley, Karen, and Barbara Hinckley. *American Best Sellers: A Reader's Guide to Popular Fiction*. Bloomington & Indianapolis: Indiana University Press, 1989.

Holden, Stephen. "At the Movies: Rob Reiner Films Unusual Teen Drama." *New York Times* (8 August 1986): C8.

Horsting, Jesse. "Stephen King Gets Behind the Wheel." *Fangoria* (August, 1986): 34-37.

Hunt, Robert. "King of Horror." St. Louis (August, 1986): 40-41.

Jedinski, Lars. Stephen King Page. 26 June 1996. Netscape. Available at: http://members.aol.com/larsj/menu.htm.

___. E-mail message to Michael R. Collings. 27 June 1996.

Kanfer, Stefan (with Cathy Booth). "King of Horror." *Time* 6 October, 1986: 74-83.

King, Stephen. "Brooklyn August." *Io* 10 (1971): 147.

___. *Carrie.* Garden City, NY: Doubleday, 1974.

___. *Christine.* New York: Viking, 1983.

___. *Creepshow.* New York: NAL, 1982.

___. *Cycle of the Werewolf.* Westland MI: Land of Enchantment, 198?; New York: Signet, 1985. As: *Silver Bullet.* New York: Signet, 1985.

___. *Danse Macabre.* New York: Everest, 1981.

___. *The Dark Half.* New York: Viking, 1989.

___. "The Dark Man." *Ubris* (Spring 1969); *Moth* (1970): [n.p.].

___. *The Dark Tower: The Gunslinger.* West Kinsgton, RI: Donald M. Grant, 1982. Rpt. New York: New American Library, 1988.

___. *The Dark Tower II: The Drawing of the Three.* West Kingston, RI: Donald M. Grant, 1987. Rpt. New York: New American Library, 1989.

___. "Do the Dead Sing?" *Yankee* (Nov. 1981): 138+. Rpt. as "The Reach" in *Skeleton Crew* (New York: Putnam, 1985): 487-505.

___. *Dolores Claiborne.* New York: Viking, 1993.

___. "Donovan's Brain." *Moth* (1970): [n.p.].

___. *ES [IT].* Trans. Alexandra von Reinhardt. München, West Germany: Heyne, 1986.

___. *The Eyes of the Dragon.* Bangor, ME: Philtrum Press, 1984. Rpt. New York: Viking, 1987.

___. *Firestarter.* New York: Viking, 1980.

___. *Four Past Midnight.* New York: Viking, 1990.

___. *Gerald's Game.* New York: Viking, 1992.

___. *The Green Mile, Part One: The Two Dead Girls.* New York: Signet, March 1996.

___. *The Green Mile, Part Three: Coffey's Hands.* New York: Signet, April 1996.

___. *The Green Mile, Part Two: The Mouse on the Mile.* New York: Signet, May 1996.

___. *The Green Mile, Part Four: The Bad Death of Eduard Delacroix.* New York: Signet, June 1996.

___. "Harrison State Park '68." *Ubris* (Fall 1968): 25-26.

___. "Here There Be Tygers." *Ubris* (Spring 1968): 8+. Rpt. in *Skeleton Crew* (New York: Putnam, 1985): 135-139.

___. *Insomnia.* New York: Viking, 1994.

___. *IT* (typescript). March 1986.

___. *IT.* New York: Viking, 1986.

___. "King's Garbage Truck." *The Maine Campus* (20 February 1969-May 1970).

___. Letter to Michael R. Collings. 3 March 1986.

___. Letter to Michael R. Collings. 31 March 1986.

___. "Love Those Long Novels." *Adelina* (November 1980): 9.

___. "The Mangler." *Cavalier* (December, 1972). Rpt. *Night Shift*. Garden City NY: Doubleday, 1978: 76-95.

___. *Misery*. New York: Viking, 1987.

___. "The Raft." *Gallery* (November, 1982). *Twilight Zone Magazine* (May/June, 1983): 32-46. Rpt. *Skeleton Crew*. New York: Putnam, 1985: 245-270.

___. "The Revelations of 'Becka Paulson." *Rolling Stone* (19 July/2 August 1984). Rpt. in *Skeleton Crew*. Santa Cruz, CA: Scream/Press, 1985. Excerpt from the unpublished novel, *The Tommyknockers*.

___. *Rose Madder*. New York: Viking, 1995.

___. *'Salem's Lot*. Garden City, NY: Doubleday, 1975.

___. "Silence." *Moth* (1970): [n.p.].

___. "Slade."´ *The Maine Campus* (11 June 1970): 4; (18 June 1970): 4; (25 June 1970): 5; (2 July 1970): 5, 7; (9 July 1970): 5, 7; (23 July 1970): 5; (30 July 1970): 6; (6 Aug. 1970): 5.

___. *The Stand*. Garden City, NY: Doubleday, 1978.

___. *The Stand: The Complete & Uncut Edition*. New York: Doubleday, 1990.

___. "The Star Invaders." Triad/Gaslight Books, 1964. [Mimeographed chapbook].

___. "Stephen King Comments on *IT*." *Castle Rock* (July, 1986): 1, 5.

___. *The Tommyknockers*. New York: Putnam, 1987.

___. Untitled poem ["In the key-chords of dawn"]. *Onan* (Jan. 1971): 69.

___, and Peter Straub. *The Talisman*. New York: Putnam, 1984.

Koontz, Dean R. *Dark Rivers of the Heart*. New York: 1994.

___. *Dragon Tears*. New York: Putnam, 1993.

___. *Intensity*. New York: Knopf, 1996.

Lally, Kevin. "Here's A Movie to Stand By: Stephen King Adaptation Is a Sleeper." *The Courier-News* (Bridgewater, NJ) (8 August 1986): G1.

Lansdale, Joe R. "Art of Darkness: A Conversation with J. K. Potter." *Twilight Zone Magazine* (February, 1987): 61-62.

Lilja, Hans-Ake. E-mail message to Michael R. Collings. 27 June 1996.

Louka, Loukia. "Horror Stories Have Staying Power: The Dispatch Talks with Stephen King." *Maryland Coast Dispatch* (8 August 1986): 11, 73, 80, 86, 88.

Michael McAlcin. E-mail to Michael R. Collings. 22 June 1996.

McDowell, Michael. "The Unexpected and the Inevitable." *Kingdom of Fear: The World of Stephen King*, ed. Tim Underwood and Chuck Miller. Columbia, PA: Underwood-Miller, 1986: 83-95.

McGuire, Karen. "The Artist as Demon in Mary Shelley, Stevenson, Walpole, Stoker, and King." *Gothic* 1 (1986): 1-5.

Maryles, Daisy. "Hardcover Bestsellers: These Were the Year's BIG Sellers." *Publishers Weekly* (14 March 1986): 29-31.

Masera, Andrea. E-mail to Michael R. Collings. 22 June 1996.

Mewshaw, Michael. "Novels and Stories." *New York Times Book Review* (26 March 1978): 13, 23.

Miller, G. Wayne. "King of Horror: His Career's in 'Overdrive' as He Directs His First Film." *Providence Sunday Journal* (3 August 1986): I1, I3.

Morin, Hugues. "Stephen King Books in French." E-mail to Michael R. Collings. 23 June 1996.

Mutter, John. "Paperback Top Sellers." *Publishers Weekly* (14 March 1986): 32-36.

Pareles, Jon. "Film: By Stephen King, 'Maximum Overdrive.'" *New York Times* (25 July 1986).

Podhoretz, John. "Stopping 'It' Before It's Too Late." *Insight* (25 August 1986): 68-69.
"Publishers Weekly's 1990 Bestsellers Fiction." *Publishers Weekly* (March 8, 1991): 19.
Ratliff, Larry. "Stephen King's 'Maximum Overdrive' Spins Its Wheels." San Antonio, TX, 1986.
Reed, Rex. "'Stand by Me'—A Corny Kids' Caper." *New York Post* (8 August 1986): 22.
Schweitzer, Darrell, ed. *Discovering Stephen King.* Mercer Island, WA: Starmont House, 1985.
Shapiro, Susin. "One Picture Is Worth a Million Words." New York *Daily News Magazine* (13 July 1986): 8-11.
Somtow, S. P. "A Certain Slant of I: Stand by Stephen King." *Fantasy Review* (October, 1986): 11, 16.
Spruce, Christopher. "Stephen King: The Critics' Non-Choice." *Castle Rock* (December, 1985): 1 4.
"Stephen King." *Bookwire.* 29 May 1996. Netscape. Available at: http://www.bookwire.com/BookInfo.Author$153
"Stephen King." In *Contemporary Literary Criticism*, ed. Dedria Dryfonski. Detroit MI: Gale Research, 1979: 309-311.
Stephen King Krant. Utrecht, Belgium: Uitgeverij Luitingh, 1986.
Sullivan, Jack. "Ten Ways to Write a Gothic." *New York Times Book Review* (20 February 1977): 8.
Todorov, Tzvetan. *The Fantastic: A Structural Approach to a Literary Genre*, trans. Richard Howard. Ithaca, NY: Cornell University Press, 1975. [Original French edition, 1970.]
"Top Fifteen National and Local: C. W. Hay Bookseller." 13 April 1996. Netscape. Available at: http://www.maple.net/cwhay/bestloc.html
"Top Fifteen National and Local: *USA Today* List." 11 April 1996. Netscape. Available at: http://www.maple.net/cwhay/bestusa.html
Underwood, Tim, and Chuck Miller, eds. *Fear Itself: The Horror Fiction of Stephen King.* San Francisco, CA: Underwood-Miller, 1982; New York: Signet, 1984.
___. *Kingdom of Fear: The World of Stephen King.* San Francisco, CA: Underwood-Miller, 1986.
Verniere, James. "Twilight Zone Review, 1986: Film." *Twilight Zone Magazine* (February, 1987): 47-49. Mention of *Maximum Overdrive* as one of the "bombs" of the year.
Wager, Walter. "More Evil Than a 15 Foot Spider." *New York Times Book Review* (24 August 1986): 9. Review of *IT*.
Wiater, Stanley. "The Stephen King Phenomenon." *The Valley Advocate* (21 July 1986): 30.
Williams, Scott. "King: Doctor of Dementia Has Directorial Debut." *The Red and Black* (University of Georgia) (24 July 1986).
Winter, Douglas E. "John Coyne: A Profile." *Fantasy Review* (October, 1985): 12-14, 33.
___. *Stephen King: The Art of Darkness.* New York: NAL, 1984; revised and expanded, 1986.
Wolfe, Gary K. "Strange Invaders: An Essay-Review." *Modern Fiction Studies* (Spring, 1986): 133-151. Review of King criticism.
Yarbro, Chelsea Quinn. "Cinderella's Revenge: Twists on Fairy Tale and Mythic Themes in the Work of Stephen King." *Fear Itself: The Horror Fiction of Stephen King*, ed. Tim Underwood and Chuck Miller. San

Francisco, CA: Underwood-Miller, 1982; New York: Signet, 1984, p. 63-73.

Zieman, Mark. "When Buying Rare Books, Remember: Go For Stephen King, Not Galsworthy." *Wall Street Journal* (14 January 1985): 6.

INDEX

155

MICHAEL R. COLLINGS

Thinner (King, as "Richard Bach-man"), 9-11, 18, 38, 46-48, 50, 52-53, 63-64, 118-119, 130-132, 136, 138, 140-142
"This Guy Is *Really* Scary" (King), 12
Thomas, Ross, 10
Thompson, Jim, 11
...*tick...tick...tick* (film), 125
Time (magazine), 144, 147
Todorov, Tzvetan, 30
Tolkien, J. R. R., 18, 113
Tolstoy, Leo, 84
The Tommyknockers (King), 10, 12, 26, 33-43, 47-48, 51, 53, 67-69, 100, 104, 113-114, 120-121, 130-131, 133, 137, 139, 141-142, 144
The Tommyknockers (TV film), 14, 38-39, 144
Tonto, 117
"Tough Talk and Tootsies" (King), 11
Triad Publishing Company, 6-7
"Trucks" (King), 8
tulpas in literature, 27
"Turning the Thumbscrews on the Reader" (King), 12
the turtle in literature, 20, 31
Twain, Mark, 87, 97
Twilight Zone (TV show), 12
Ubris (magazine), 103, 109-110
"The Ultimate Catalogue" (King), 12
"Umney's Last Case" (King), 140
"Uncle Otto's Truck" (King), 10
Underwood, Tim, 10, 12-13, 78, 89-90, 100, 144
"The Unexpected and the Inevitable" (McDowell), 90
United Artists, 117
University of California, Riverside, 15
University of Georgia, 92
University of Maine, Orono, 7-9, 12, 17, 92, 103, 106-107, 110, 115-128
University of Massachusetts, Amherst, 11
University of Vermont, 92
The Unseen King (Blue), 13, 90
Updike, John, 93
Us Magazine, 9
Valley Advocate (newspaper), 78

vampires in literature, 28-30, 85-86, 88
Van Buren, Abigail, 119
Van Dyke, Dick, 104
Van Hise, James N., 10, 13
Verne, Jules, 42
Vietnam War, 119
Viking, 50
Village of the Damned (film), 86
Virginia Beach, Virginia, 12
"Visit with an Endangered Species" (King), 9
vurderlaks in literature, 29-30
Walpole, Horace, 90
The Waste Lands (King)—SEE: *The Dark Tower III*
"The Way Station" (King), 9, 132
Wayne, John, 127
"The Wedding Gig" (King), 9, 140
"Weeds" (King), 8
Wells, H. G., 42, 113
werewolves in film, 27
werewolves in literature, 28-30, 85
Westfield State College, 100
"What Ails the U.S. Male" (King), 11
"What Is Death? What Is Goofy?" (Brooks), 145
"What Went Down When Magyk Went Up" (King), 11
"When Is TV Too Scary for Children?" (King), 9
"Where's the Playground, Susie?" (Glenn Campbell), 123
"Whining About the Movies in Bangor" (King), 12
Whiting, Leonard, 116
The Who (musical group), 113
"Why I Am for Gary Hart" (King), 10
"Why I Was Bachman" (King), 11
Why We Dance (Goddard College program), 104
Wiater, Stanley, 78-79
Widmark, Richard, 127
Wilbur, Richard, 118
The Wild Bunch (film), 124
Wild in the Streets (film), 123
Williams, William Carlos, 109
Winston, Wynde, 104, 116
Winter, Douglas E., 10, 78, 91, 93, 101, 146
Wizard and Glass (King)—SEE: *The Dark Tower IV*

ABOUT MICHAEL R. COLLINGS

MICHAEL R. COLLINGS is a professor of English in the Humanities Division of Pepperdine University, and director of Creative Writing for the Communication Division; he has been on the faculty at Pepperdine for over seventeen years, teaching composition, creative writing, and literature. He has published a number of books on science-fiction and fantasy topics, including:

Piers Anthony, Brian Aldiss, and a series on King—*Stephen King as Richard Bachman, The Many Facets of Stephen King, The Shorter Works of Stephen King* (with David A. Engebretson), *The Films of Stephen King, The Annotated Guide to Stephen King,* and the original edition of *The Stephen King Phemonenon* (all through Starmont House, now Borgo Press);

Reflections on the Fantastic and *In the Image of God: Theme, Characterization, and Landscape in the Fiction of Orson Scott Card* (Greenwood Press);

Cardography, a bibliography of Orson Scott Card (Hypatia Press);

The Work of Stephen King: An Annotated Bibliography & Guide (Borgo Press, 1996);

And scores of chapters, articles, and reviews in periodicals and anthologies, such as George Beahm's *The Stephen King Companion, The Stephen King Story,* and *The Unauthorized Anne Rice Companion;* Stephen Spignesi's *The Shape Under the Sheet: The Complete Stephen King Encyclopedia;* Bill Munster's *Sudden Fear: The Horror and Dark Suspense Fiction of Dean Koontz,* and others.

In addition, Dr. Collings has published several books of poetry: *A Season of Calm Weather* (Hawkes); *Naked to the Sun* (Starmont); *Dark Transformations* (Starmont); *Matriz* (White Crow); *Haiku* (White Crow/Zarahemla Motets); and *All Calm, All Bright* (White Crow/Zarahemla Motets). He is also a consulting editor for *Poet Magazine.*

9 780930 261382